SPIRITUAL KNOWLEDGE

PEKKA ERVAST

SPIRITUAL KNOWLEDGE

Pekka Ervast Series
I

THEOU SOPHIAN EN MYSTERIO

AATMA

Published by Aatma
www.aatma.fi

ISBN 978-951-8995-21-3

Translated by Lauri Livistö
English and Sanskrit proofreading and corrections by
Ilkka Castren
Cover photo by Pirjo Aalto
Preface and back cover text by Seppo Aalto
Layout by Lauri Livistö

The translation of this book was supported by the
Kulmakoulu foundation.

FOR THE READER

This book is a collection of lectures held by Pekka Ervast (1875-1934) in Helsinki, Finland, between 1917–1929 which cover human super-senses (extra sensory perception), clairvoyance, yoga meditation and spiritual knowledge which enable exploration of the afterlife. The lectures were written in shorthand and are not edited to a literary form, but the characteristic style of the speaker is retained.

Pekka Ervast was aware of the invisible world since his childhood and strived consciously to reach God. He had a spiritual experience at the age of 21 which made him an independent investigator of the invisible world. For the next 38 years his contribution was remarkable. He lectured weekly (at first especially in neighbouring Sweden), was the founder and General Secretary of the Finnish section of The Theosophical Society, Founder-President of the Finnish Rosicrucian Society, edited magazines Omatunto ("Conscience"), Tietäjä ("Sage") and Ruusu-Risti ("Rosy Cross").

Highlights from his remarkable literary work include clarifying the spiritual essence of the Finnish National epic Kalevala, work in the field of Christian occultism explaining the sermon on the mount and the five commandments of Jesus to seekers of truth, translating sacred texts of oriental religions into the Finnish language, and clarifying the inner path of Freemasonry.

Ervast was the founder of the first masonic lodge in independent Finland, and a 33 degree founder-member of the Finnish section of the International Order of Freemasonry Le Droit Humain. He was also the Founder-President and Grand Master of the Finnish Rosicrucian Freemasonry.

PUBLICATIONS IN ENGLISH:

The Mission of the Theosophical Society, An open letter to Theosophists the world over (1921)

The Sermon on the Mount , or the Key to Christianity (1933)

"H. P. B."; Four Episodes from the Life of the Sphinx of the Nineteenth Century (1933)

The Esoteric School of Jesus (1979)

Astral Schools (ebook 1979)

The Key to the Kalevala (1999)

The Divine Seed: The Esoteric Teachings of Jesus (2010)

From Death to Rebirth (ebook 2017)

From Death to Rebirth (audiobook 2018)

Spiritual knowledge (2018)

www.pekkaervast.net

TABLE OF CONTENTS

I

HUMAN SUPER-SENSES

When we want to explore man's senses, we must foremost of all keep in mind that man himself is not the same thing as is his physical body. He is the psyche, the soul, the spiritual being, the sentient being that lives in the body and uses the senses as kind of tools through which he can gain information from the surrounding world, and function therein. We as theosophists cannot imagine, like people who have no knowledge of this matter, that human as a spiritual being would be one with his senses; for we know that man himself is a spiritual trinity – a spiritual being comprised of three aspects. He is a willing, knowing and feeling centre of consciousness, who uses the senses as he lives in his body in this material world. Senses belong to his bodily being; they have evolved therein. Through them he gains information from the material world; through them he also guides his actions in the world of matter. We must keep this in mind. A human is a spiritual trinity, and the aspects of his being are, according to this old psychological categorization: will, feeling and knowledge.

When a human as a conscious spiritual being lives in this physical world he uses five senses; and also two others, which have not yet evolved in all people and which we will discuss more later on. These senses have gradually evolved in man's physical being, and are still evolving. They are not

9

the ready results of creation, but have developed gradually, which also has been proved by scientific research. We must mention that the order in which the senses have been categorized in evolutionary terms differs in scientific and occult understandings. This is due to the fact that scientific research studies only the coarse physical being of man, and so reaches not further back in its studies than the genesis of this coarse physical body. Whereas the occult science also takes into account man's invisible physical body, the etheric body-double, and alongside the physical evolutionary history studies man's earlier stages in a world which was not similar to this visible physical world, but was etheric, super-physical. Occult science teaches that on this globe man evolves through seven root races, and in every root race man develops one sense. In the first root race hearing evolved, and touch, the sensation in the second. These races were not yet physical, but super-physical, etheric. Not until the third root race, which was the first physical one, can be reached by scientific research. Therefore concerning the evolution of the senses does science state that sensation was the first to develop, and hearing after it. Science acknowledges that hearing can exist in very early stages of development, but claims that it is sensation that is the first sense after all. Occult science instead states that in the third root race – in which scientists place the evolutionary beginnings of both hearing and sensation – does a human start to develop sight. And that at the end of this root race man was already in occult terms a fully rational, seeing, hearing and feeling being. In the fourth root race taste developed, and in the fifth, which we are now living in, smell.

Then there are those two senses that yet have not truly evolved into bodily senses, but will later on develop as such; the so-called sixth and seventh sense. In the sixth root race all people will develop a sense which can be called a "sympathetic sense", and in the seventh race, the last of the physical senses, which can be called "telepathic sense". We all shall have seven senses, of which the preceding five are already relatively evolved. The last two senses are dormant; they function in some ways, but compared to the others they are in a state of slumber. After this brief description we can better depict all senses and their occult development; they will be seen in a way that on the other hand they are some sort of channels through which man as a spiritual being receives information from the surrounding world. On the other hand they are tools of interaction, which one must have to be able to live and act in the world that surrounds him.

When we think of man in this first root race, we know from theosophical teachings that man did not yet have a proper ability for thought, i.e. sense of personalized self; but instead his human sense of I was still in state of development, and thus the human spiritual life was very primitive. Man was without form, a rather nonspecific blob or a cloud; he was like a mere aura. He did not have a human body. What purpose did it serve to his sense of I that he developed hearing in this first root race? This hearing was no physical hearing, there was no development of the physical ear – which could start only in the third root race – but this hearing was more of a spiritual and mysterious quality. In this invisible world man was a being like an aura, whose inner life was so vague that he had but one goal. What was this goal? In this elementary state his only endeavour was to keep on existing. This took almost all of his efforts. It takes a lot of effort even now, but back then man didn't have any other interests. So it was a rather limited life, rather primitively limited; it was just that that he remained in existence. And that awareness of existence was in no way romantic, it was only such that he somehow remained in balance, upright, together. The world back then was like a waving ocean, and if one was careless or unable to remain upright, it would not have just swallowed and sunken him, it could have penetrated and disintegrated him. It was a grand world of sound waves. If one as an occultist would now try to position himself according to the first root race and understand it, he would get in his consciousness an image that the world had been kind of creative sound, a word of creation. And one who then had been incarnated into that world must have tried to remain upright and together. That task took all his life. And the ability which he developed, which helped him remain upright and not be disintegrated was "hearing". In that world one also developed the sense of balance, which is connected with the ear. It is a scientific fact that ear is connected with balance. This ability evolved in the first root race. It was not hearing in such a way we now consider hearing. Man lived in a world that was like a storm of sound waves, which surrounded him and would have knocked him over if he didn't have the ability of balance. And when he used this ability and tried to remain upright, there was something in him that sounded.

Each sense has both its positive and negative, active and passive aspects. The passive aspect of a sense is the so-called sensory reaction, a reaction of the sensory organ to the stimuli of the surrounding world. A positive aspect is that when a man manifests himself through his senses: he knows, thinks, wills and feels. We can call the sense's passive, negative side "reaction", and the positive side "action". Thus the passive side of hearing, i.e. reaction, is remaining in balance, and the positive side, i.e. action, is creating sound in oneself. For in that first root race there was no particular sound as we now understand it. Man did not have any such senses by which he could have received or created sound, but the whole of his being sounded.

The next sense was touch, which evolved during the second root race. Touch is also a very old sense. It is not difficult for us to comprehend the sense of touch of the second root race, as it was close to the physical sense of touch. In this root race, when man was still without a physical body, the functioning of this sense was that he reacted to hot and cold. It was the sensation of hot and cold. So the reaction of touch is to hot and cold; and if we want to be scientifically accurate we can only discuss heat, so therefore we say that the reaction is heat. It is not difficult to understand what is the action of this sense. Man has this quality that he flees from and tries to avoid excessive cold, as well as heat, because in him there is a very specific inner warmth, and he cannot bear too great an opposite to his own warmth. Therefore he flees from excessive heat or cold and searches for temperatures suitable for him. And the ability that awakens in him through this attribute is movement. When man started to sense hot and cold, he started to move at the same time. So the action of the sense of touch is movement; and such is the evolution of man's senses from the perspective of his super-physical being.

As we now begin to study the evolution of the purely physical senses, it's good to keep in mind that before this man had developed the sense of touch, and alongside it mobility. I will not guarantee which physical sensory organ is the first to have evolved; but both touch and hearing are the primitive, primary senses. It is therefore that all living creatures have developed the sense of touch, and also have the ability to move. But at the same time are they balanced, so touch and hearing together develop physical balance, even though there not yet be an outer ear.

Sight was the third sense to develop in man, and only then did he truly become man, as then did the selves of mankind incarnate: the so-called manasaputras, sons of intellect, the true spirits of men, who until then had stayed in inner worlds, for they were unable to incarnate in that earlier primitive super-physical mankind. They incarnated in the third root race, and thus human thought awoke alongside human sight. Thus we come to the conclusion that the first truly human ability is sight. And if we ask what is the reaction of sight, what is its inner quality, then can we naturally say that it is thought. Its reaction is thought, which explains the world that is seen. The action of sight on the other hand is the thought that creates action in the world. We call the passive and receiving thought reaction, for thought only becomes active when man himself wants to create something. Thought is passive when it only explains the surrounding world. Man sees, notices something from the world surrounding him, and accordingly gets an image

13

in his mind. That is the thought which is the reaction of sight, but the action of sight is corresponded by external action.

We notice that when man has obtained these first three senses, he actually has almost, as it were, accomplished himself as a spiritual being. He can somehow manifest a part of his soul, for these three senses correspond with man's trinity: will, feeling and knowledge. Then he is perfect as a living being. He *is*, when he is in balance – *moves* and *takes action.* When he reached these three actions, – is, moves and acts, – then was he complete, and then the physical body originated due also to his higher self, his human constituent part, being born into that body. – Only then come the other senses, which only expand man's range of action as he *is, moves* and *takes action*, but they do not add to him anything essentially new.

When it is said that taste evolved in the fourth root race, we can ask what is the action and reaction, the inner quality of the human soul that simultaneously developed in man? The fourth root race lived on the continent of Atlantis. And when we think of that Atlantean race and its life in the context of what is described in theosophical literature, we know that man had a great problem to be solved which man did not solve back then, and which has since then been, and still is a problem of mankind. In the fourth root race man developed taste, and at the same time the human soul was given the problem of good and evil to be solved. For the passive side, i.e. reaction of taste, is the choice between good and evil, and its action is taking action regarding that choice. Reaction is that something with which he distinguishes good from evil, and action that choice according to which he takes action. This ability developed in man during the fourth root race. – Let us state in passing that when talking of good and evil, there are people who would not use those terms. They discuss taste in other meaning as well. They say for example: "It is good taste which tells a man what is good and what is bad." This is rather simplified thinking.

Now we live in the fifth root race, and it is smell that
has evolved, and is still evolving in this race. So we ask:"
What is the spiritual quality and ability we must develop
in conjunction with this sense? – What is its corresponding
spiritual quality, the problem that must now be solved?" It
is the problem of health and sickness; that is connected with
this sense. If we clairvoyantly study mankind's evolution,
we note that sickness did not exist as much in those ancient
times as it does now. In this fifth root race man has developed
a more perfect nervous organism, and this is why they are
also more susceptible and receptive to diseases than they
were before. In this race mankind is facing the question of
health and sickness. What else is mankind thinking these
days than how to remove illnesses and make mankind as a
whole more healthy and strong? Mankind has been given
this problem, but we haven't solved it yet. None of us is
yet completely freed from what we call sickness. Even if
a great Master would incarnate on Earth he would also
be susceptible to all the infirmity that is intrinsic to us.
Therefore the problem of health and sickness is the reaction
of smell, and the action is overcoming sickness.

Then we come to the sixth root race, which must develop
a sympathetic sense, this peculiar ability to sense sympathy
towards a fellow human. The effect of this ability is most
clearly visible in youth. When one is young, a boy or a girl,
then some people from the opposite sex affect others in a
very magnetic way. And the one who has the most magnetic
influence on a particular person becomes the object of his
or her love. It is this dormant sympathetic sense which
dictates whom to fall in love with. It is a mysterious and
unconsciously functioning sense, like a great force of
nature, and therefore it is said: one cannot know why he
falls in love with him or her. This sense also tells a person
who is hostile towards him. – This ability may have been
physically more evolved in the past than it is now. When we
clairvoyantly observe the atlantean times we notice that men
had a sense alike this one. People were astrally clairvoyant,
even though this clairvoyance was not such as it will be

when clairvoyance in a more exalted significance evolves in man; then will this astral clairvoyance be in conjunction with more profound senses. These factors are now evolving into the sympathetic sense. – But then, in the ancient times, when sight was less evolved than now, this astral clairvoyance was of a very primordial quality and it was connected with something akin to the future's sympathetic sense. These future senses, sixth and seventh, are peculiar in a way that they are very close to man's actual super-senses, which the sixth and seventh root-race will develop. So in the future, when they will evolve, man's spiritual life will also develop his astral and mental abilities so that they can easily be mixed with each other. When the future man develops clairvoyance, then maybe it will provide a few surprises. Especially in the sixth root race there will be a rather proximate danger, the symptoms of which we can already notice. When man develops super-sensory abilities, they are alike senses which can react, but he cannot control them. They are only passive reactions, which we call mediumship. In the sixth root race mediumship will be a common phenomenon. Even though man would not be clairvoyant then he will have a great deal of mediumship. Unless we are scientifically exact mediumship is considered to be everything that is unknown to the five senses. And the problem that the sympathetic sense presents us with is of a new kind. We are already facing that problem, and we cannot solve it. It is the problem of love and hate.

And then we can also tell what the problem will be in the seventh root race, when a telepathic sense will evolve. We can say that in this race, whose inner tone will in essence be goodness , the problem will be the influence of good and evil on men, or as we could say – white and black magic – or generally speaking just magic. Then the positive side, the action of the sense will be hypnotism and suggestion, man's influence on other people. One will then know every moment what is his influence on others.

– Senses, their reactions and actions are as follows:

Sense	Reaction (passive)	Action (positive)
Hearing	Balance	Sound, pronunciation
Touch	Heat	Movement
Sight	Thought	Action
Taste	Good and evil	Goodness
Smell	Health and sickness	Health
Sympathy	Love	Hate
Telepathy	White magic	Black magic

We must now notice that we have been discussing solely about the physical senses, and not at all of the so-called super or spiritual senses. Therefore we ask now: "What are those spiritual senses, those astral and mental super-senses?" We answer this question right away: They are not any new physical senses. Only seven physical senses will evolve, which we have discussed previously. And when super-senses begin to evolve in man it means that he starts retracting his physical senses, to focus more on this world he has discovered. With physical senses he has learned about the surface and exterior of this world, but as astral and mental senses awaken he turns inward and studies the world closer than before. Therefore we must not think that astral clairvoyance would be the sixth sense, and that mental sense would be the seventh sense. This claim is inconsistent because the sixth and the seventh sense are physical senses that evolve in mankind in the future, whereas astral and mental senses are super-physical senses which evolve alongside physical senses. They are always used to study inner worlds; with them we study this world from the inside, in a more profound way. So when we discuss astral senses we must not confuse them with these seven physical senses.

When we talk about super-physical senses we can distinguish three different varieties: astral, mental and buddhic senses. It is so that an astral sense is always corresponded by a physical sense, as are mental and buddhic senses alike. Man has possessed these physical senses as long as he has been a human being; the talk of astral and other super-senses means only that the power of the physical senses is turning inwards.

When are talking about astral senses they are commonly called clairvoyance, and it is a reference to the fact that astral sensing is seeing. Anything one would sense astrally he would try to interpret this sensation in imagery. One who has experienced something astrally knows that this experience was manifested in images. When a man sees something astrally, it appears as if some sort of a painting or a movie: he sees a painting with just one surface, but with life in it. And therefore we can understand what some occultists mean when they say that clairvoyance differs from ordinary sight in such a way that it reduces dimensions. When in this visible world we have three dimensions, these occult philosophers say that in the astral world we are reduced to two dimensions. There are only two dimensions; it is just like a surface. This is an occult truth, so that many esoterists may well describe the astral world as a world of two dimensions. On the other hand it is so that while describing the astral world many occultists call it a world of four dimensions. – If you have read my book "Mitä on kuolema?" ("What is death?"), you know that in it I speak of the astral world as a four-dimensional world, which is also an occult truth. It is a notable issue that the astral world is a world of both two and four dimensions. You can say that it is a two-dimensional world, but if you wish to be scientifically accurate, you can talk about four dimensions. – What is the effect of the fourth dimension? It is a rather peculiar dimension. When we want to describe three dimensions, we say that they are formed by thinking of three straight lines facing each other in a perpendicular manner. There we have three dimensions, and if we were to add a fourth dimension to them, it would mean that against these three perpendicular lines a fourth line would be drawn, which would be perpendicularly against them all. We know that we cannot imagine this. But what does this fourth line, which doesn't exist, really affect? For all practical purposes this fourth dimension reveals the whole object, it sort of "opens" it. If we take under observation an object, for example a table, in the four-dimensional world, then this fourth dimension, which perpendicularly intersects the three dimensions, will show this object from all sides simultaneously, it spreads it to a single surface in its entirety. The fourth dimension makes it so that the table withholds no secrets from our gaze. In three-dimensional world a table always has one side that we cannot see, but when we look upon it with astral sense, along the fourth dimension, it spreads out as a surface, and reveals all its secrets. This is figurative speech for in reality an object does not spread out when we are looking at it astrally, even though it reveals all its secrets as if it were a surface. Our gaze does not penetrate inside the object, so therefore we can talk about the astral world as being two-dimensional, and say that astral sight is seeing in two dimensions.

When we want to distinguish and discuss more comprehensively about astral senses a good aid is a pattern, which depicts senses according to different states of matter. Occultly categorized matter has seven states, three physical: solid, liquid and gaseous; and four etheric, which are called first, second, third and fourth ether. The solid state corresponds with earth, liquid with water and gaseous with air. Now in this pattern these states of matter correspond with senses as follows: earth corresponds with touch, water corresponds with taste – taste is the sensing of all fluidic substances. Air corresponds with smell, and the ethers, in ascending order: first sympathy, then sight, hearing and telepathy. These senses are also divided into different groups, so that the first lower ones are called tactile senses and three upper ones vibratory senses. Nonetheless so that the three lower ones are the true tactile senses and the fourth, sympathy, is a hybrid between tactile and vibratory senses. This pattern is good to keep in mind because when astral senses start to develop in man, they will do so according to states of matter. They can start their evolution from whichever stage but they can always be categorized like physical senses, even though not according to physical senses, but states of matter.

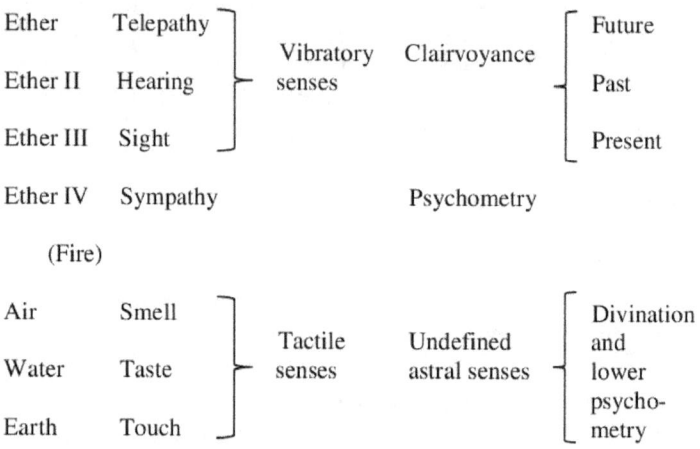

Ether	Telepathy				Future
Ether II	Hearing	Vibratory senses	Clairvoyance		Past
Ether III	Sight				Present
Ether IV	Sympathy		Psychometry		
(Fire)					
Air	Smell				Divination and
Water	Taste	Tactile senses	Undefined astral senses		lower psycho-
Earth	Touch				metry

What is characteristic for astral senses is feeling, for when one starts to receive astral impressions, a vague feeling arises in him. Astral sensing is always about sensing some kind of emotion, for the astral world has as its base tone what we call emotion. The astral world is not alike this physical world, even though it is described as such. It is said that there exist landscapes, animals, plants etc. like in the physical world. This is all only seemingly so for the reality is very different. The world that presents itself in these images has as its base tone emotion and the power of emotion; and therefore its forms are totally dependent on the feelings and thoughts of people and other living beings. This physical world cares not much about thoughts and feelings. No matter how much we think and feel that this city should be different, it doesn't change. In the astral world this is a totally different matter. It differs from this world in such a way that it is susceptible to the effects of emotions; so that when one looks upon a scenery and wishes that it would be different, it will then transform. From our own dream-life we know that in the dream-world our surroundings are not as certain as is the physical world, but can suddenly transform depending on our imagination.

When the *lower astral senses* awaken in man they can be felt as undefined astral sensitivity and primitive psychometry, which enables one to somehow predict the future and divine. I mean divination as all sort of activity that is not guessing, but contains real information; meaning every kind of divination, be it by using cards, eggs, alcohol, hands, etc. For this is caused by awakening of the lower astral senses, and one of its aspects is this sort of lower psychometry. This means making astral sensing easier by some kind of method. It is noticed that it is easier if the one you are divining for can be touched. If you can hold the hand you are divining for, that slight touch has a psychometric effect. Often the mere vicinity of the person being divined for has a psychometric effect. This is a case of the kind of astral sensing when an astrally sensitive person notices the other person's spiritual atmosphere i.e. the aura. This aura effects in such a way that something from the person's future can be noticed and solved. This sensing can take such a form that one thinks he is seeing some sort of colourful phenomena. It doesn't necessarily mean any greater clairvoyance, for these lower senses show us just these kinds of colour-phenomena. When one starts to comprehend the astral world he starts to see colour-phenomena without any physical reason. Astral seeing is just seeing colours.

When psychic abilities develop further, man will develop a *true psychometric ability*, and that is a rather strange thing. We have seen examples of true psychometry when the English Mr. Peters visited here. He gave us many examples of it. He would take an object in his hand, and the first impression thereof was either sympathetic or antipathetic. And when he overcame this first impression, he would see an image, which had nothing to do with the object itself. He would for example be given a watch, and he would get an image of the deceased who had in time owned that watch. The watch gave him that astral, psychometric clue which led him to the departed, not in the spirit-world, but to the memory which exists of that dead person. Some aura of the dead person has adhered to the watch, and the psychometric has the ability to know what caused it. He takes the watch in his hand and sees: there's a lot of blue, and then he knows that the deceased was a wonderful person, a spiritual person. When he contacts the aura of the deceased in this manner he can then say: the person who owned this watch was like thus and thus.

Man will not reach true astral sight before the higher astral senses have developed in him. These three higher senses are all some sort of clairvoyance. First of these higher senses, the one that corresponds with and deepens the physical sight, is clairvoyance in the present. It is farseeing that corresponds with physical sight, but is not limited by location. It can see as far as wanted in this physical world.

Another higher sense is clairvoyance to the past, and that corresponds with and deepens the physical hearing. This is also a kind of farseeing, but of a kind which travels as far back in time as is wanted. – But when clairvoyance reaches its full potential in this greater significance it is linked by a third aspect, which advances the highest physical sense, the telepathic sense. Then man will reach a state of unlimited sight regarding past, present and future.

We can categorize the senses like this but a full clarity of their quality can be obtained only through experience. When these senses evolve further, more profoundly in mankind, like that of the aforementioned sight to the past, then we can for example study history in a totally new fashion. We already have an example of this kind of study. There is a professor in America, whose wife possesses great psychic abilities, and he has published a couple of books in which his wife tells of her experiences. For example when she was in Egypt she told the most wondrous things about the pyramids. When this ability awakens in man, he can then study history in an absolutely new way. How much more reliable is this kind of research than memorizing from books the conclusions of historians? In future it will be researched how things have really happened.

Lastly we try to briefly describe what mental senses are. As astral abilities are like seeing pictures, so is mental sensing a kind of hearing. It is not physical hearing, it is sensing as if by hearing. And this means that this world, which astrally sensed is seen as a surface, a painting, is with mental senses revealed a step deeper. When we astrally see a colour, and when this is joined by mental sensing, we will then also understand what it means. This "understanding" is not exactly the same as we usually mean by understanding. Here we understand something in a way that we make observations and then make conclusions based on what we have learned from them. For example when we astrally see something blue in a person's aura, we say: "Ah, I've heard that blue colour in aura means this and that." But another clairvoyant while observing the same phenomenon might say: "But that is red!" – There is no guarantee whether a clairvoyant has really seen correctly unless a mental sense has also awoken in him, which will tell him: This thing means this and that. Seeing a colour is not the point, but that the colour-phenomenon itself says: I mean this and that. Mental sensing means exactly this; mental ability enables a person to understand, and that understanding is based on the object itself. It is not like physical understanding, which is based on conclusions made according to facts, but it is understanding which comes to man instantaneously, without any material cause, without previous thinking, and says to him unquestionably how things are. I hope that I have managed to portray even a slightest of picture what is meant by astral, mental and physical senses and sensations.

II
OCCULT KNOWLEDGE

A man who lives this physical life can usually say: we live in two different and contradicting worlds; sensory and intellectual; that is: the visible and the invisible world. Man is called upon to uphold balance, harmony, between these two worlds, to actually build harmony between these two worlds. His task is not to give in to his senses, but it is not his purpose to live solely in the invisible thought-world either. Man lives not only in his own thoughts and according to his own principles, but he must stand between these two worlds and build a bridge between them, and keep them together in balance and harmony. Man's task is not to give in to the senses but to uplift and purify them; to fill them with thought and thus create a new world out of this visible world. Not in such a way that he would use his own visions as a model, but so that he learns from the invisible world and rectifies the visible world accordingly. He will also notice that one who wishes to create harmony takes upon a new stand on life. He will take a stand that there always will be praise and thankfulness in his soul; he will praise God and be thankful for everything. Good and evil will thus lose their contradictory meanings. In this new outlook on life evil does not exist in the same way as it used to. It will not make him suffer. Evil is not about man facing accidents or something being taken away from him. Evil is himself becoming so weak that he will do evil; that

25

he will become so weak that he gives in to his senses. He must not give in blindly to his senses but as a man stand as a mediator between the thought-world and the sensory world.

Now we might ask must one keep in mind these general advices which dictate what must not be done? You must not succumb to your senses; you must become a master over them. But you must neither surrender to your thoughts, for then you will become bitter. You must not succumb to your own reason and see evil in everything, because then man himself defines by his own reasoning what can and what cannot exist. Man assumes a position as a judge outside of life, and says: "This and this is sin", and tries to suppress his urges. He begins a struggle in which he will lose his strength and in the end become weak and lifeless. If he hangs too much on to his own sanctity and exemplarity he will in the end face spiritual death. That danger exists and therefore one must stay in the middle; not succumb to his own senses or thoughts but create a balance between them. Then can one relate to everything in life in a new way: he will demand nothing but takes a thankful stand regarding everything.

We notice that all great people, the great redeemers of the world have said and taught that: "Your soul is precious; your soul must lose its shackles and strive upward. Do not give in to the senses."

This first rule is of negative quality for it says what one must not do. If we wish only to philosophize and theorize, if we wish to be very logical we might become one-sided and say: it leads to fatalism if man cannot do anything himself but everything is just fate. I will become a fatalist if I must take the stand that I not demand or expect anything but just be thankful for everything; become calm, will strive for nothing, will not be touched by anything, do nothing out of my own initiative, be passive and let life show what must be done and will not falter. Is it really so? If I would inspect this in a simple, one-sided way I could come to the conclusion that it is so. It is fatalism that we must not demand anything from fate. This is taught in some religions, like Islam: everything is kismet.

We know that the occult, theosophical understanding of life is not the same as fatalism, is not the same as kismet. It is instead a positive and active attitude to life, without rules; it is very positive, it is strength, it is more like theosophical principles, more like guidelines of life. When we start to seek the mysteries of life then theosophy answers: man is the master of his destiny. Theosophy does not teach, nor did the wise teachers of old that man would be a slave to his fate. Man is the master of his destiny. Man is not subject to karma in a way that he would always be its slave, that all he does would be under karma's rule and would be his own karma. Destiny has not set things this way. Karma is not always that a man faces an accident, a seeming wrong, for that which can face a person is not always his own karma but it can also be nature's karma, a people's karma.

Fate is like before the eyes of every person. Everyone has had to ask: is this my karma; is it my karma that I will face an accident? If we ask this question it is not always absolutely sure that it is personal karma. It might be that if one is powerful enough a personal being he might have personal karma. But most of the time it's nature's karma, a people's karma, because men must partake in collective karma. If instead one has good personal karma he will be saved from danger, he will for example not be hit by a bullet but he will be saved. Therein is witnessed good personal karma; karma is shown in that deliverance. Or one is saved but has a strange urge to throw oneself back into the same danger and is killed; therein is witnessed bad karma. Let it be remarked that the concept of fate is not so easily understood than one might first think. Fate is a complex matter and we will focus on it now.

When we hold on to the idea what the occult and theosophical understanding of life says: no fatalism, – then what is this new strange attitude on life, what is so remarkably positive about it, what is this new stand on life? It is not a negative thing, it is not about what should not be done, but it is what should be done; not about what we are not allowed, but what we are allowed to do. One might think negatively and start fighting against his desires and sins through asceticism and self-torture. But if one were to succeed in this he would become proud of his own achievements, would become mentally proud so that he would be on his way to a spiritual death. There is a right way by which we can be relieved from bitterness and pride, and that is humour. If your soul is bitter or spiritually proud try to laugh; try to laugh at everything in yourself and others for how ridiculous we are in our pride and roaring bitterness. We would be rid of that if we could apply the salt of humour, the "Attic salt". With humour we could get rid of bitterness.

Then what will man's positive relation to life be? How must one relate to life? There is an occult advice. We remember that formally speaking man is a manifold being, and as is said in theosophical literature he has not only a body in a physical sense but also has supernatural bodies outside the sensory world, invisible vehicles. We have to understand that man has not only this visible physical body in this material life but he is a being of more complexity. We know from theosophy that he has also other vehicles which can also be called material.

When we now want to give some kind of instructions for life we must not give these instructions from below; not give them regarding any sensory instruments. If one wants to give instructions that are valid regarding life in its entirety then they must not be given for any specific instrument, but they must originate from higher levels of being. But to be able to give instructions from which higher knowledge can be obtained one must look at human life and composition with higher, inner eyes. How can we come up with advice that would be effective in all vicissitudes on the long journey of life?

Let us presume that man would have such an eye with

which he could gaze deep into the mysteries of life or that there would be a person like this close to us and we would ask him: "What advice could you give us?" Then this wise one might say: "You must be human on every level of matter, in every vehicle, in every world; you must always live as a human being and retain your humanity. Your positive task is to become human and retain your humanity." This is a general, mysterious instruction which we cannot understand unless we concentrate on its practical meaning.

When it is said that a person must on every level, in every vehicle, in every state become and be human, we ask: "How is it that we should live in the physical world in order to be human?" This is answered by this wise person: "It is not enough that you have this human form. If you wish in reality to be what you already seemingly and based on appearance are, then you must retain your humanity." How is this possible? We know it must be something positive. How can we be positive and retain our humanity in this visible world? It is achieved by working. This is the positive advice which is valid in this physical world. Man must work. He is in this visible world in order to work. But as he is working he must constantly keep in his soul an ideal which is much higher than the work he is currently performing. He must not lose sight of this ideal. He must not become a machine which thinks nothing but work and fulfilment of his duties. If he has a task which life has given him he must carry it out as well as possible. This is his positive task, this is his responsibility. But at the same time he must think about a more wonderful future: what is this greater work which he wishes to do, which would be even more wonderful for him?

Almost all people are in a position that they have dreary work. If the quality of a person's work is unpleasant then he has to think that he must perform it even better and more skilfully. If he is an artist he tries to portray his subject always as well as possible, but at the same time he will idealize in his mind a work of art which will be a thousand times better and wondrous than he is currently working on.

One must always keep an ideal in his mind and think how it can be fulfilled. When he is working on what is at hand he also thinks and plans how he would have wanted to do it in an even better way.

Laziness is the greatest wrong in this physical world. One must not become lazy; one must not give in to mental laziness. He who does not plan how he could do all his work in a better way is lazy. No one can blame him and yet he can, when spiritually considered, be lazy. Man must be positive like a businessman who constantly plans bigger and bigger businesses.

A worker has a small pay; he works hard and thinks: "Oh, how I wish to be paid better!" This is not a wrongful thought. It is laziness if he does not think like this, but he must be careful not to do wrong and must not blame others. He is mistaken if he says: "The wrongdoing of others inhibits me." If he permits this kind of bitter thought in his soul he will start to drift downwards. He must take a grateful, open stand on life: "I don't have to be satisfied with what I have but must plan how I can better do my work; how I must be skilful and gain much power over the material world in life." That is the art of living. One must not become bitter but he must strive even more.

When we look upon a man from a higher plane, through the Creator's eye, then what do we see? We see more than the physical body, we see more than the astral body. We might have an idea of the astral body as a multi-coloured cloud in the aura. But when we start looking with higher sight, with the Creator's eyes, what do we see? We see what the poets see – for they have a supernatural sight. We see that that there is an animal within every man; this in one, that in another, one has a peacock, another a wolf, yet another a bear. This animal is hidden from the physical world. Usually it is said that it is in the astral world but only the Creator's eye can see it. When a man has this astral animal in himself, when in every man is hidden an astral animal, then what will his salvation be in the astral world?

What was the advice we received from the wise man? "Be human in every world!" We must transform this animal that is hidden within us into a human; it must be assimilated into man. When an animal hides and lives in the heart of man it must merge into him. What must this animal become? First its eyes will change human-like and then it will gradually become human altogether and finally become one with man.

That is the goal of this advice on life. It is not about afterlife, but about how a living human being must act. So how can we learn a way to humanize our astral animal? We answer this: We can learn this from nature. – We know that also in nature the occult purpose of the animal kind is to become human. How does this happen? It happens so that an animal becomes fond of a human being; love awakens in its soul and this love can transform it to human. – There are other ways as well but this is one of them. In this case the animal's soul becomes fulfilled with love towards a human. That is the rule in the animal kind. An animal rises to become a human when it learns to love. – So a human must also learn to really love if he wishes to transform his astral animal into a human. If he learns to love then lust in him will vanish; it is purified by love. This is the rule, way and advice which nature teaches us, and of which man can get a glimpse of when he learns to faithfully love another, as it is supposed to be in marriage. For marriage must be a union between two people who are faithful, who strive to this kind of union and uphold it throughout their physical lives. In every religion man is taught to hold this matter sacred. Nevertheless, this kind of marriage is rare in practice for we know that often he fares differently in life; his marital life is not spiritual. But we see and understand what the occult meaning of marriage is, what is its occult significance. Its inner purpose is that the animal in man could become transformed into human. For an animal can become human when it is faithfully loved. If the animal in man does not learn to love faithfully it will remain an animal – and is manifested as lust. If it learns to love it is saved no matter the sort of lust. We know the great power of personal love. If two people could really love each other so that they would be faithful to each other, really wished only good to one another, would really serve each other and would really be joined together then would lust disappear from them. This is proven by the experience of life. This experience is not achievable by only a select few but is the lesson of family life that faces man. One must learn to faithfully love another human being. When he learns this then will his animal become human. – We could discuss this greatly but it is best that everyone would just think about this themselves as the wise old ones have taught. It is said that if one wishes to grow spiritually one must have at least one friend, a human, a partner, whom he can love faithfully. He must be allowed to personally love at least one human being so that he will say: this person is the joy of my life! A man who strives for the narrow path in this physical life must become physically and sexually absolutely pure. He must have this kind of gift to offer to the Master, to God. He must be in love and purified so in his love that he no longer has an animal within him. He must be totally pure. – Or he must have at least one such life in his past in which he has been pure. This is like a reference to what life could be.

But there is more to man than this astral life and the astral instrument. We know that behind and inside man's astral body is, theosophically speaking, the mental vehicle, the thought body. This is an ordinary observation to an already clairvoyant eye. But when, with the Creator's eye, we try to concentrate on man we notice that there is something else in him. – For what do we see when we look with the Creator's eye? If we look with the Creator's eye and concentrate on what we see, we see something like a flower, a tree, a plant. We see something belonging to the vegetable kingdom. Physically we see a human, astrally an animal. But when we mentally concentrate on man we see a plant, for as a thought-being man is like a plant, a flower, a tree. Then we ask: how can man also mentally be human? How can this plant or flower also become human and be human?

If we examine man's soul we understand that it truly is

going through a transformation. We see that in the thought-world man's soul is just like a tree, or some other plant, but when his consciousness opens mentally then out of that plant will emerge a wonderful, human-like nature spirit – objectively speaking as it were. Looking through the Creator's eye we see that in a forest there can be a tree inhabited by a nature spirit, which might step out of the tree and show itself. In a similar manner we may see with the Creator's eye that also from the human soul in this thought-world, which is like the vegetable kingdom, might come out such a nature spirit shaped and looking like a human.

When can this happen? When he remembers the rule that he must be human also in the thought-world and when he wishes to accomplish this. What does this mean in practical terms? Man must become a seeker of truth in a true way. He must seek the truth by working positively on himself. – Many people talk about seeking truth but real seeking is something totally different than the usual conception regarding it. Seek truth above all else. This is what man must do for such is his essence. The physical life and the world are such that man spontaneously receives information. He sees the world, gets images of it in his mind and concepts awaken in him. And when concepts awaken in him he will then understand general laws of nature. The whole of his logical thinking has its origin in sensory functions, just like materialism states that man's intellect is nothing more than what he has perceived with his senses. The whole of man's thought-life starts with him sensing the outer world and forming pictures and concepts of his perceptions. This is one side of the matter but it is not yet seeking in a true significance. True seeking of truth is that man gathers information, not only with his senses, but by other means as well. Man must not seek truth only by his senses. Scientific seeking of truth is based on senses and scientists invent machines to enhance the potency, accuracy and sensitivity of the physical senses. So the scientific seeking of truth is not true seeking for the scientific community does not seek truth and knowledge through other means than the senses and worldly intellect. The true seeking of truth is done by other means as well.

What does it mean then that man must seek truth in other than scientific ways before he can become human in the mental world? Man has plants and trees in his soul – and if he at the same time is happy and calm they will at first become beautiful flowers and herbs. – But when a person wants to become human also in the mental world he will at first seek truth through meditation and philosophical intuition. And when he seeks truth in such a way and arrives at certain conclusions then concurs that a human is born into the thought-world; a human is born in the middle of the flowers and trees.

But we can go yet deeper; the Creator's eye can reach even deeper. It sees something else behind this mental, vegetable world. What does it see? It sees a crystal palace, or a rock palace. For deep within the human soul is like a palace of rock. In deeper essence man is like in the mineral kingdom which is formed by a geometric, lifeless world. It is not of the animal or vegetable kingdom; it is like a lifeless world, the mineral kingdom. It is like a crystal palace, like New Jerusalem, or we could as well say it is like a golden egg. How will this become human? What does it mean that man must be human also in this mineral kingdom, and what is this mineral kingdom, this crystal palace? It is really nothing else than man's sense of self. This whole palace of rock, the New Jerusalem, the golden egg is man's I-ness. The self of man, the I, is yet not human. So man must also become human in his self and retain his humanity in it.

Then what does this mean? We can understand this in some way. If we look through the Creator's eye at the man who is going through this transformation we see the golden egg breaking, and out of it comes a Creator who creates worlds. That man must be human also in his self means that his self must become a Creator. He must no longer be in a passive relationship to life but he must become positive. He must get a chance to create life, be a Creator. He must become a Creator who creates worlds. – When a man does positive work and breaks off his shackles, when he creates a world of his own, then this I will finally break its golden egg and become human. Then man will be born as a Creator and create worlds.

III
CREATIVE KNOWLEDGE

Occult knowledge can be compared to external knowledge with the difference that occult knowledge deals with different areas. First glimpses of that knowledge are comparable to making observations regarding this physical world. The first level of occult knowledge is comparable to the observation which one makes based on the fact that he can move in this physical world and select the areas he wishes to make observations of.

The second level of occult knowledge is that we make observations and select them. When we look at this physical, bodily life we notice that our life is not limited only to making observations and moving around, for besides doing that we can also choose our observations. We notice that our life is much richer than mere passive existence. It is not reduced only to external life. It is not only that life passes by us and we just observe and move. We do not only make observations but take part in life itself, we act and work in order to be able to achieve something in this world. The actual content of our lives is that we work, act, talk and bring about changes in the surrounding life. That is our real life. – We notice that even animals do so; for example they build nests for themselves. So we say that the most important and noticeable part in the life and existence of man in this visible world is that he takes part in life, that he is some kind of actor in life, some kind of creator, for man also always creates something.

Occult knowledge is also creative knowledge. It creates something new, it is not lifeless observation, it is creation. This definition might be hard to understand, but when we study occult knowledge we will understand what is meant by it. It means that because in this visible world life is action one must act in this physical life; and living this physical life he must find a corresponding level also in the occult knowledge.

Occult knowledge is at first seeing, making observations. "Seeing" is such a limited word, for seeing in the occult world is not similar to seeing with physical eyes. The word "seeing" is used in lack of a better word. It could also be called mental perceiving. On one side it is seeing, for the lower aspect of occult knowledge might be described as seeing, but really it is moving in the invisible world.

The next level in occult knowledge which one must reach when travelling the occult path corresponds with real life and action in the physical world. If we consider a little what action in the physical world includes we can say: action in the physical world always includes giving life to a mental image. If we do something in the physical world it is as if we were fulfilling some kind of mental image that is within us. We cannot act unless we have an idea of the work we wish to do. If thought is focused on a certain direction then action towards that direction realizes the image in an external way. So action is crystallizing a mental image.

But we also discuss the motives of action, for one can have different motives in his actions. He might act for example from the sense of responsibility, but he could also act from exalted love. Behind it there is an image, a thought which descends into the visible world, a thought that comes alive in a man's action. What then corresponds to this in the life of occult knowledge, what corresponds to it in creative knowledge? The occult world is not about coming up with ideas of our own, for if we should ourselves make up what we must know then that knowledge would be worthless. That would be no real knowledge. It is not a question of anything like that when we are talking about real knowledge. Occult knowledge is not something that a man would have to make up of his own accord, but instead he must be able to find what really is in that world. It is just like in this visible world when someone like Columbus starts off to seek a new land. He knows that there is a new land and goes on to find that. Gaining occult knowledge is also like that. One must not make up anything new but find what already exists. One must know how to move and wander, to make observations and thus he must know how to find what already exists. – If one can read then he can make certain observations when a book is placed in his hands. If he can only spell then his possibilities for making observations are still slim, but if he can read well he can make more observations and can choose what to read. If the book is in a foreign language he does not understand it straight away, but he can learn this strange language and then his possibilities for making observations increase.

Such is also the occult world. One who can make observations in it can also select them and say: "I wish to examine that", or also: "I don't care about that", – if he understands what he sees. It is very important that we understand what we see, for on that is based the ability of occult reading. It is also the key which leads to the next level, which is that what we see, observe, might enter us and awaken some action within us. It might come alive in man and tell of itself what it is. For example if we see a vision then it will itself say: "This is what I mean."If we have an incident like this then it will be born in man and as if roll out of him and tell of itself what it is. It is really also like hearing, although "hearing" is really just a physical word.

I have had a certain small experience of this topic which will enlighten the matter. I have had this always when I have heard Mrs. Annie Besant speak. Mrs. Besant is a very peculiar and gifted speaker, undoubtedly one of the world's most impressive speakers. When I heard her speak it aroused in me a certain strong impression which echoed in my soul and left an echoing memory of her speech, so that when I took up her printed speech and started reading I did not see the words but heard the voice, I heard how she spoke. As I was reading I heard her speaking along. When I had physically heard how she spoke this speech influenced my reading and it made an immediate impact like speaking of a real person.

One can make an observation like that and I wish to compare this to occult knowledge, which is akin to that, so that when we see, then it is as if that particular thing itself would were in our consciousness. It is like that subject, that occurrence, this being would explain itself. However that happens within ourself. We know this and we trust this information but it is not something our mind made up. It is living information, it creates itself through us.

People who study the spiritual world describe the details in different ways. Their information is not necessarily wrong but they look at things from different angles, so one who wishes to get a reliable idea of the spiritual world should compare the descriptions of different seers, for living sages are limited, imperfect beings and their knowledge is always comparable to their level of development. Yet there may be such sages whose knowledge is thoroughly creative knowledge. I wish to emphasize the term "creative knowledge" for even though no knowledge is non-creative, the third level of occult knowledge is true creative knowledge. We must remember how much more vivid and truthful information is in that other world than in this visible one.

If I meet someone for the first time I cannot yet say that I would know him. If I have passed by him I might describe his appearance, and if I happen to be a skilled physiognomist and can judge his characteristics by appearance then I might describe him in more detail, but I might still be wrong. And even if I get to spend time with him and learn to know him better he might still remain a closed book for me. I know nothing about his inner life, his soul and spiritual life until he tells me of himself. And however skilfully I usually could judge him and make conclusions in reality I would not know him until he would tell me something about himself. – This is comparable to the third level of occult knowledge for it is there that a being or object tells us about itself. It is born in us, it is itself crystallized within us. This is much more real than the previous kinds of occult knowledge.

When we have reached so far in the occult knowledge that all beings in the invisible world themselves reveal their inner thought-essence so that we can make the right conclusions and participate in them, we face yet a higher level of knowledge and our knowledge will then be even more profound and clearer, even more truthful than before. That knowledge is at the same time action; that is the real creative knowledge. – In the visible world, in life itself we can notice two different kinds of action. Man acts either self-consciously or unconsciously. When one knows what he is doing we call that self-conscious action, that he is in his action absolutely free and not forced by any inner or outer factor. We see only very rarely action that is absolutely free. Man's action is almost always derived from some kind of compulsion, some kind of necessity. Some part of his action can be free but most of the time it is dictated by necessity. This necessity may be the desire living in him. Free human action is very rare although everyone is free to some extent. I can for example freely decide to lift this glass. We can make this kind of distinction regarding human action, we can talk about self-conscious and unconscious action. Most of the time our action is unconscious, only a small percentage of it is self-conscious but this portion must grow.

What compares to this in occult knowledge? All this information we gather in this new world , the spiritual world, the world of consciousness, must come alive in us or else it will remain self-unaware. We strive for this information to create itself in us. We ask for nothing else than that the world would create itself within us. We have no choice. We might say, as long as we do not know about this, that the world cannot create itself in us. But to reach knowledge we must wish the world to be born in us.

But when we come to the highest, most profound kind of occult knowledge we no longer are satisfied with the whole world of phenomena in effect in us, but we wish that that which is behind everything, God, would create itself within us. We wish that God which is innermost in us, the cause of life itself, the one which is common in everyone, that this God would create itself in us. We wish to become the Self and that man could be conscious about the Self. This means that man's inner Self, which is God, would create itself within us. Not that the world would reflect in us but that God would create itself in us and man would become Creator. – All wise ones have taught that man must seek God and find Him. Only then begins the divine life.

Now we wish to give a short overview of this and compare the information in theosophical literature concerning the path of purification and the path of initiation. Theosophical doctrines mention these paths and they say that man must first journey through the path of purification and then reach the true path. Spiritual forces already affect on the path of purification but not until the path of initiation do they come truly alive in man. The path of purification is a preliminary part in the spiritual development of man when he yet does not come self-aware in the spiritual world but lives in the physical waking consciousness. It does induce certain alterations in the physical waking consciousness which affect man's spiritual being, but it is not until the true path that the spiritual life becomes self-aware in his consciousness and is then transformed within him into a self-aware path. The path of purification does in secret some alterations in the higher vehicles of man, does some preliminary work in them, but man himself lives in the physical waking consciousness because he is yet not conscious of anything but the physical world.

The two qualities that must be reached first on the path of purification has two are, by their Indian terms: *viveka* and *vairāgya*. Viveka is the ability to discern the real from the unreal, and vairagya is dispassion towards what is unreal. These first two qualities of the path of purification correspond to the purification of the brain. When a man tries to travel the path of purification he practices with these two qualities the purification of the brain and discerning insight. His experience of viveka and vairagya are of philosophical nature. A man who has reached these qualities has not only sought truth with his mind but also with his soul and his heart. He has discovered that life, existence, is eternal; he has gained knowledge of the divine world. Practising viveka and vairagya means in fact that a man has learned to know something of the God within and now he wishes to fulfil that within him even though he still is bound to the worldly, ephemeral life. And now as he is bound to it he feels tired of life. Now he wishes to be able to give his life to the Master for he feels within that his own life is nothing, it is like a burden. A notable quality in a disciple on the path of purification is that his motives have changed. He lives only because God wants him to live. He wishes that his life is devoted to God, that he could live in front of God, before the eyes of Christ. This is the first step on the path of purification. It affects so that the disciple does not care about the visible life; he is tired of life.

Then there follows on the path of purification those so-called six virtues: *shama,* calmness, the control of the mind; *dama*, the control of the actions; *uparati*, renouncing the wrong natural impulses; *titikshā*, enduring patience; *samādhāna*, the concentration of mind on one subject, and *shraddhā*, reverent faith. And these correspond with the six levels of spiritual knowledge. These six virtues help a man to overcome evil in himself. When he practices these qualities he will notice that it is his own evil which prevents him from living before God. – How for example could evil thoughts live in God? – Therefore a man must practice these six virtues and this means that he must control his thoughts and feelings, to become patient in the events of life. These things he must learn. He must learn to seriously think or

43

else he cannot control his words and actions. He must learn to defeat evil. He will not defeat evil in himself unless he can observe and control his thoughts. – One does not learn to move in the invisible world until he has faced the so-called dweller on the threshold and defeated it. The dweller is his own evil which faces him and he must overcome it. – On the preparatory path he must learn and develop the six virtues so that he could learn to overcome evil in him.

The fourth level on this preparatory path is *mumukshā*, the desire for liberation i.e. salvation, and only then does the part of occult knowledge turn up when man himself can understand creative knowledge and when the spiritual world will itself reveal its secrets to him.

A person must always learn to inwardize one's awareness into within himself. Samādhāna is that he learns to control his thoughts and can meditate. He takes a subject to study upon and he must know how to think about it, to focus and concentrate on it so that it becomes clear to him. Only then will the subject tell about itself, will reveal itself. Man must know how to meditate so that the subject will gradually explain itself. This meditation will develop shraddhā, faith i.e. trust. Faith and trust develop in man in that there are masters and there is knowledge. This evolves to mumukshā, the desire for liberation, that man wants to be free of all illusion, wants to be free.

There comes so powerful a desire for truth that it it feels as if something in him would break; he feels that he cannot exist unless he unless he can arrive at the knowledge of truth. He must know what is the truth.

This is all still the preparatory path. And the peak of the preparatory path is that the desire for truth becomes so strong that nothing can resist it. A person downright breaks his own soul. And after this kind of effort from the deeps of the soul there awaits enlightenment which leads to initiation. The path of preparation ends up in initiation and this means that a man for the first time gains knowledge that there is something true, and feels it and knows it.

In the first initiation a man becomes aware of the spiritual world and this corresponds to the first level of occult knowledge we spoke of earlier. The second part of occult knowledge is that a man learns to move in the spiritual world and select his perceptions; and this corresponds to the second initiation. – The first initiation actually deals with the physical world and it means that a man in this physical consciousness becomes aware of the divine spiritual world. – The second initiation is that when a man steps out of himself to the spiritual world as an independent citizen. He enters it and lives in it. In the third initiation, which is a mental initiation, the initiation of a genius, a man attains to creative knowledge of the invisible world. Then he arrives to a connection to all the secrets of this world.

Here we must note that when talking about the third initiation as the initiation of the genius, it is a reflection of the truth that the great geniuses of the world, the great artists are men who have undertaken true initiations. The inspiration of a genius is not a laughing matter. It is not hereditary or the grace of God but depends on the fact that this human soul has strived and experienced so much that he has gained knowledge of the spiritual life, that the world itself tells him its secrets. If he for example walks on a meadow or watches the trees of a forest they will tell him things, they will reveal their essence. This is occult knowledge. This is the ability to hear what nature tells a man. And this ability depends upon the fact that he has striven before, searched the truth with enormous efforts so that he now has gained this ability with which he can listen to the language of nature.

The fourth initiation or the first great initiation is that God creates himself in man, that God is revealed again in man. This is the arhat initiation when he is lifted on the cross. This is the initiation of the crucifixion in which man, from an occult viewpoint, dies. This is the apotheosis, the triumph of occult knowledge. Man becomes Christ so that he can always live in Christ, but like St. Paul says: "It is no longer I who live, but Christ lives in me." This means that man has given up his own personal self, has died and

45

Christ has taken the place. This is the highest form of occult knowledge we have discussed herein. When this state is reached, God lives in man. When a man has reached this state that God lives in him, that Christ is born – and not only so that Christ is merely born but that Christ lives in man – then can we say that a totally new path of knowledge begins. Now begins such a life of knowledge and such possibilities of knowledge which will raise him to the manhood of Christ and the perfection of Christ, which will raise him to the Christ initiation when he will become one with the Logos. We know that then he has been raised to the initiation of the master which is so high that it usually takes seven incarnations before someone who has taken the arhat initiation can take the master initiation, even though he already has died from his personality and lives for the benefit of mankind. This is the sign of a person on the path of true initiations, as the path of preparation has its own signs.

First a man lives for himself and then he starts to live for humanity, for all people. The first reflection of this is the weariness towards life that appears in the beginning of the preparatory path when a man is tired of working only for himself. He wants to work for others. On the path of preparation he might still mistakenly make calculations benefitting only him but in the first initiation this new outlook on life becomes so clear that he cannot be mistaken anymore, even though he might still be weak and deficient in its practical applications. He cannot be mistaken on the basic meaning of life; he cannot be wrong on the basics of life, that is: to serve or not to serve? He has vowed to eternally serve mankind, to serve God. For example he can be wrong regarding the means, but only when he has taken the fourth initiation a totally new life will begin.

IV
SKILLED CLAIRVOYANCE

Clairvoyance is a complicated, difficult issue; everyone who has the slightest of experience, or has dealt with this subject knows it. Clairvoyance is at times called a new sense, a sixth sense. At times it is called some kind of super sense. It is also said that a clairvoyant person can see another person's soul, even his spirit, and can study this person even to the inner core.

When these kinds of definitions are given we understand that this is a really difficult question, for we hardly would like to admit that a man's spiritual being, his self as a spiritual being would be something that is perceivable by senses, that it would be a material being. So the question remains what is clairvoyance, if with it is possible to perceive things that are not perceivable using regular senses. And on the other hand it is said that clairvoyance is exactly about perceiving things that are in themselves phenomena, even though they are super-sensory phenomena. It is said that a clairvoyant person can see another person's aura, i.e. a sphere of colour around him, which means we are dealing with sensory phenomena. – Then clairvoyance would be a new sense, a sixth sense.

When it is said that with clairvoyance it is possible to see through walls we understand that it is some kind of sense. But if with clairvoyance can be seen whether a person is

47

good or bad, has he gone through a certain evolution, then it seems that it is something which perceives intangible things. – So we ask what clairvoyance really is? – This is a complicated and an abstract problem to solve. And if we now wish to try to analyze and clarify this it is done to the best of our skill but is not an exhaustive presentation.

Because clairvoyance is called a new sense, the sixth (and seventh) sense, when it is paralleled to man's known senses, it is good to first take a look at this question from the viewpoint of the senses, to think a little about our known senses.

We have, like it is usually said, five senses. A modern day psychologist can talk about other senses as well; he then takes into account all sensations in connection with the human organism but does not bring forth anything particularly new. Therefore we usually state that man has five senses, which are: sight, hearing, touch, taste and smell. These five differ in their functions and therefore we talk about five senses. We also know that since from ancient times according to ancient traditions these five senses have always been connected with different elements in nature. We have been told of four elements: earth, air, water and fire, and then the fifth one which is more mysterious, which is ether. We know that our senses are paralleled to the elements in such a way that earth is corresponded by smell, water by taste, air by touch, sight by fire and hearing by ether.

Thinking of these correspondences we right away notice that they have some sort of logical connection. For example when we say that taste is connected with water we notice that no taste can exist without moisture. If we place a dry object in our mouth it has no taste until it gains moisture, when again smell is connected with earth, i.e. solid matter. We say that smell is seemingly connected with air – we talk about gases – but if we put, for example, a wooden object in our mouth it has a taste, but it is more like a smell. – Touch is connected with air, – even though we say that touch becomes more apparent with a material object. But we know that we also feel hot and cold. – Sight is connected with fire, i.e. light; this is so obvious that it needs not to be discussed. – But it sounds even more mysterious when we say that hearing is connected with ether. When old nations connected hearing and ether they were close to truth, we notice this from the fact that hearing and ether have a profounder content. For how can we think about only hearing when discussing music? If music was only the influence of air to our ears then how could we understand music, for after all music is felt most of all within the soul. The airwaves that resonate in our ears are so soulful that we ask how could we people create such airwaves unless hearing would be like a mysterious inner sense?

If you ask any composer he will say that he hears the notes first himself. If he composes a song he does not think about making airwaves vibrate at such and such length, nor so that he inputs emotion or thought into airwaves but he hears inside him heavenly music when he for example hears a song being sung. It affects in silence, on another plane; then he manifests it here. All instruments are imperfect; they cannot manifest what he hears for he has heard more delicate sounds. He might for example hear three sounds between notes c and d instead of two. When he has a keen ear for music he hears more sounds within him than he can physically manifest. They are hearing sensations and they are connected with another element than air, because he cannot produce such sounds he wishes, for example, with a violin. Therefore we might understand at least with our intellect that hearing as a sense is dealing with some other element than air.

The occult theory is that we really only have three senses which later on manifest as seven senses. At the moment man has five senses but he will have seven before he is a physically perfect human. But these seven senses are variations from the three main senses, which are sight, hearing and touch. They are the three original senses. Smell and taste are already some kind of variations between these other senses. Both taste and smell are clearly connected with touch. Taste cannot be thought of without touch and neither can smell, for us to be able to smell anything it must touch our olfactory nerve. Smell and taste are thus only differentiations of touch.

From this we understand that because we will have seven senses – seven is the base number of nature, all wise ones have noted this – so can we undoubtedly understand that the two senses which will develop are neither any new, primary senses but some kind of alterations from the main senses. And if we take an old and known example we notice that even such a sense like smell might as well have appeared occult, mysterious when it still had not developed in all men but only in some.

For example let us imagine that in Atlantis, when there did not yet exist the sense of smell, there were a few children in a forest where they had not been before. One of those children, a small girl is advanced in such a way that she already has a little bit of this sense of smell. The others know nothing of this. This small girl then says when they are sitting on grass: – "Oh, there are beautiful roses somewhere here!" The others say: "There are no roses here." – "There sure are." – "How do you know this?" – "I know and see it with my nose." – "What nonsense is this, to see and know with your nose?" And the other children would not believe it. They went walking and behind a rock everyone noticed roses. Then they wondered that the girl knew this, for she had not been there before as none of them had.

The sense of smell undoubtedly appeared then as an occult sense, a supernatural ability. When it occurred among grown men it was considered humbug and such a person was denounced as an imposter. It was said that he had found out earlier about the fact he now claimed to know about.

We know that in our time there are people who are called clairvoyant. They can know about things from which they have not had information via ordinary physical senses. We consider them as imposters or supernatural beings. – The previous little example shows us that it is not a supernatural thing, but it is like some kind of foretelling. When it starts to rain a few drops come first – when a new ability evolves it develops first in a few people.

Let us first see in which order the senses we now have developed according to occult studies. We know that mankind's history is divided into five root races. In the first root race, when man lived on the etheric plane, hearing developed, in the second developed touch, in the third sight, in the fourth taste and in this fifth smell. In the sixth root race the sixth sense will develop, and in the seventh the seventh sense will. Those who have studied occultism know that our physical world is divided into seven categories, or put otherwise: materiality appears in seven different states. First is the solid matter, earth, the next is water, third is air i.e. gaseous state. Then comes the fourth which is already ether, light ether, which is in connection with our sight. Then come even higher types of ether which are of four kinds altogether.

When we think of the races of mankind and the evolution of senses during these times, we notice that these senses have developed in such a way that mankind has as it were descended and come to this lowest level, and is now climbing back up. For always when considering seven, three are on one side, fourth is the lowest, and three again on the other side. Evolution is a spiral; we were in the fourth root race at the lowest one, and now we are ascending. Now smell has developed, and in the sixth root race the sixth sense will develop, and in the seventh the seventh sense. Are these senses yet totally non-existent? – No. – Of course the possibilities already exist in the human organism, and in some people they can be developed. I naturally cannot say what will be the names of those senses and how they will appear as bodily senses. We can only make some kind of deductions based on perceptions and experience. We do not know either to which extent they will develop in us. All we know about these coming new senses are primarily conclusions based on empiric perceptions and experiences.

If we wish to imagine a sixth physical sense we would say that it is an alteration of these previous senses. It is at the same time a compound of them but has also given predominance to one certain sense, emphasizing a certain primary sense. We can tell from the senses of smell and taste that they emphasize touch, but they also include other senses, especially sight, because in our imagination we receive an image in conjunction with a smell or a flavour; especially with smell, as in our previous Atlantean example. Our inner eye imagines an image of that which can transmit such a sensation of smell.

This sixth sense will especially emphasize sight and the seventh will emphasize hearing, although they gather also other senses in themselves. The sixth one then emphasizes sight but it is a new kind of physical sensation. – But what is sensed with it? – Madame Blavatsky tells us in The Secret Doctrine that these senses will especially make clear that matter is not solid, but it can be seen through. The sixth sense will then be such that it is knowledge, sensing about things that cannot be perceived by our five senses. Let us take an example. A person whose sixth sense is active will without doubt know and feel when a hostile being is in his vicinity, even though he cannot see it. If he knows this being already, then at the same time when he knows its presence he will receive and image of this being before his eyes. But if he has not known it before he might get false and silly images. This can also be more like "sympathetic"; he knows beforehand that a good friend will come to meet him, or that he will meet a person who will have a sympathetic effect on him, or something good will happen to him.

This is a prophetic ability, but yet it is physical sensing. It will then concern an occurrence that is approaching, which in reality already exists, but it has not yet faced the individual in question. Such will the sixth sense be. Sight is then emphasized, as is also smell. Science will probably explain that it is a sense of smell, akin to what dogs have. They have a sympathetic sense of smell, a scent, for example, of their master. So dogs already have this sixth sense to some extent, and people will have a similar one, but it will not be limited to only vague feelings; it will include for example absolutely clear visions.

One can then have such a sensation which manifests itself to him as seeing something which happens somewhere else at that time. This is so because matter is not solid and impenetrable. – All our sensing is nothing else but sensing this materiality in different forms. So the new senses will grasp matter in a new way and elicit more out of what there is. So this sixth sense will not have any walls, or barriers in the same way our present sight, hearing, touch, etc. have. – Hearing is already less limited than sight, for we can, for example, hear what is happening behind a wall although we cannot see there. So hearing sense has already more mystery to it. – The sixth sense will especially tear off many such veils that hide from us the things that happen here.

The seventh sense will have a likewise effect, but to another direction. As far as I can see it will be a rather strange and wonderful sense. It will emphasize more hearing, but other senses are connected with it. I wish to describe it with a few words. These days we people are talented in different ways regarding this sense. Someone may be very slow when he faces something in this life; he is very slow to figure out what to do. We know that the more slow a person is, the harder it is to for him to know how to act when something unexpected happens. Therefore we say that a person who knows how to act in a situation has patience and vigilance; he has all his senses about him, wide awake. And we know that these days there are professions in which this ability is especially required. No one can for example be a good soldier without good decisive skills. Nor a good businessman; none of the American millionaires have gotten rich without this ability. If we think about a person in a dangerous line of duty we know that he must be steadfast. Anyone who has rafted down rapids knows that the person steering in the aft must be cold-blooded, charged, concentrated; for if he for even a second thinks about something else they would all be in the water. It is one of the most exciting journeys a man can make, for everyone's lives are in the hands of this peculiar, nearly god-like being, who sits in the aft and to whom no-one can talk to. It is wondrous, and such vigilance is absolutely required.

I would say now that this seventh sense which man will develop is the knowledge of how to act in a given situation; an instant flash of information that comes in the form of hearing phenomenon. If such a strange thing happens that one cannot act based on intellect, then this sense would tell him: do this and that. We know that there are situations when our intellect says nothing, but a kind of perception of ours tells us what to do. Such situations are, for example, dangers. If we were to know what to do based solely on our intellect and thoughts, it would come to nothing; but our senses will guide us then. This seventh sense will be such that we know instantaneously what to do, and it will manifest especially as hearing.

So the sixth sense will emphasize sight, and the seventh hearing. We can say that the sixth sense is a sympathetic sense, and the seventh a sense of action. These are merely names we can now come up with.

These are all then downright physical senses. But they are peculiar also in another way. For when we think of the arc our evolution goes through, we notice that in the sixth and seventh race we ascend to the very top, to the point where we left. Then this world has been revealed to us both in its visible and invisible forms. At present it is not totally open to us, but in the future it will reveal more and more of its consistence and secrets. And when we have experienced this physical world in such a way, then our consciousness has already come in a natural way in contact with another plane, i.e. world.

The secrets of this physical world in its invisible side are much more numerous than what it offers in its visible form. The realities of the invisible, we could say, etheric world are numerous. And when these new senses will develop in man, he will experience much more clearly these realities that are in the invisible side of this physical world. For example what? – For example the reality that the dead always remain in this physical world for some time before moving on to the true afterlife. They are still in this ether, atmosphere, and they have a physical body, although it is made of ether. It is invisible to plain sight, but very little is needed for it to become visible to physical eyes. There are many who have seen dead people. Nothing more has been required than that the person has been in a state of quietude, sitting alone or resting in bed. That way it is easier, although there are cases when even that is not required. Then a dead person can be visible, for he is clad in a physical-etheric body. He looks like he used to, normally the way he was when he died. It is some kind of mental image of him, we could say.

Even though the dead are already in the after-world, on the astral plane, they can still strive here from thereof. Then a medium is needed, a person whose sixth and seventh senses have already started awakening; especially the sixth sense. He is a person whose etheric body has formed into such that it already has developed a sixth sense, even though it has not fully developed in the visible, physical body. A medium is a person in whom different material compositions, different states of matter are loosely attached to each other. A dead person comes to him and strives to manifest through him in this physical world. It is as if he would get substance for himself from the medium, such "ectoplasm" that he could make himself be heard, seen and touched. The medium lends so much of this substance that he could weigh half of his usual weight when measured; and he must have given also gaseous, liquid and solid substances, for the etheric substances weigh nothing. Even in his appearance the medium has shrunk to a very small size. – Such an appearance of a dead person must occur relatively soon after death, for he must still be close to this world and his interests be here.

This is all due to the sixth sense. And this sixth sense and the bodily composition, which we will have, will establish us in contact with the invisible side of the physical world. – A man in whom this sense develops will start to notice beings that others cannot see. They are not only dead people, but he will also see gnomes, water maids, sylphides in the air, salamanders in fire etc. He sees spirits of nature to which the scientists of our time laugh at. But we need only to familiarise ourselves with the traditions of old peoples, and we will know that all old peoples have told about spirits of nature. The Finnish people have especially been in contact with them, and we still have even in these days sages who are convinced that spirits of nature exist.

We also know that this sixth sense allows us to see colour phenomena in connection with people, animals and objects. – Now we must note that at present when clairvoyants are exceptions, their perceptions may differ from one another. If we have two clairvoyants a third person, then – especially if they are from different circles and do not know each other – when they look at this third person, they see in different ways. When one says: "I think his undercurrent is red", the other might say: "I see green." And we wonder what this is all about. – Scientific researchers will call it humbug. – But it is not. – The sensations of these clairvoyants are real sensations but they describe them in different ways, and that is because they are not yet experienced; their new sixth sense is yet so undeveloped. And if we ask them how does this influence them the other might say: "It makes me feel as if the person were a very sensible." He has seen the colour red. "Oh," says he who has seen green, "he is not as sensible as he is a passionate person." – And again we are confused, until we notice that the perception of these clairvoyants include the special predominant quality of that sixth sense, which is that it is a sympathetic sense. It includes some kind of conscience, and then we understand that it is affected by the feeling from the other person. If I consider myself a sensible person, whereas in reality I would live very much in my emotions, I would say about another person who also has a strong emotional life that he is a sensible person; he knows what he is doing. For us, people similar to us always seem sensible and good.

The sixth sense is still underdeveloped and it must evolve. Therefore we come to the conclusion that all senses can and must be developed. Especially when they appear mere glimpses of what will happen to the whole mankind. Therefore it is vital to develop and cultivate them, or else they will lead us astray.

V

THE SPIRITUAL CONSTITUTION OF MAN

It could perhaps be unanimously admitted that the pinnacle of human thought was reached in the Indian philosophic system of Vedanta. This system points out the final goal of human knowledge. And this goal of knowledge is union with God, becoming one with the absolute life. And in a way, like the Vedantists themselves say, man as a subject unites with the only subject which truly exists, i.e. Brahman, God. The subjectivity of a person is his inner sense of I, that which in every person says "I". We cannot step outside of this I. And when this I of ours, our subjectivity, becomes one with the only true I, or absolute self-consciousness, then is the pinnacle of knowledge attained. According to Vedanta there cannot be many manifestations of I; there can be only one ultimate I, one true subject, and that is behind all human manifestations of I. And a Vedantist says that the ātman, 'Self', of a person is the same as God. When a person becomes aware of the fact that in his spirit he is one with God, he will attain as high knowledge as is possible to attain, for then his Self consciously contains everything in existence – one has reached union with the Absolute.

This is so profound and sublime philosophy, so high knowledge, that we cannot think of any higher. When we use the word "philosophy" we do not mean any vain ponderings and empty speculation, but when we discuss

59

philosophy the word is used in its original Pythagorean sense , it is then love of wisdom. And the highest wisdom is that which is described in the Vedanta. Even if Kant has reached far in his philosophic conceptions he cannot have gone beyond the Indian Vedanta; they have solved the same philosophical questions thousands of years ago.

If we think of Vedantic philosophy these days, and such a view of life in general, which says that everything else but the one true Reality, God, is only illusion, we can see that we are facing problems of practical nature. Even if our Western mind would admit that this viewpoint is the highest in philosophy, we would still be left asking: Can anybody reach such knowledge, become one with Brahman, so that all else to him would be illusion, everything personal would be perceived as unreal? – Can a person achieve this? We are naturally doubtful. "How is it possible that I could appear outside of all existence and see everything as illusion?" – We only have to think how when facing a great agony of the soul we are face to face with the reality as it appears to us, and even if we could have imagined ourselves being in God, at the moment when a great suffering faces us we feel that we are in a different reality than the Absolute. – Then we ask: "Where is the path to Veda, to spiritual knowledge?"

It is therefore no wonder that in old India when people started to reflect they had to face this question. And yet everybody knew within himself that the unity just mentioned was the absolute solution and to which Vedanta aims at. But at the same time it was so distant that the thinkers wondered: "What is this sensible reality? Why does it have such concrete reality to it? Why is suffering so real?" – And then it is traditionally told:

There was a very wise rishi, a seer, named Kapila who solved the issue. He created a philosophical system he called sānkhya.* It means consideration, deliberation, thinking,

---

*Literally 'enumeration', from the word sankhyā, 'number'. (Editor)

reflection. Kapila appealed directly to man's intellect, to his reasoning, when he presented his system. – Now the European scholars are not convinced whether there has been any Kapila. We always start by doubting those wise ones who are said to have existed. To us they are always nothing but legend, mere myth. – Indians had a philosopher named Îshvarakrishna who wrote down the Vedanta system in an Indian fashion, very briefly. It is of course very old, it was written before Christ. It is argued whether it was written before or after the Buddha, but in any case this presentation, named Sānkhya Kārikā, is deemed very old. It is written in Sanskrit and in an Indian fashion very briefly. The same earlier mentioned monistic philosophy is expounded there in the most beautiful and accurate manner. Sanskrit is such a language that merely a few words can describe extensive ideas.

The writer of the Sānkhya Kārikā traces his knowledge all the way back to Kapila, and therefore in the text he writes what Kapila allegedly has spoken. And the scripture begins with Kapila stating: "All is suffering", – just like the Buddha – "and it is so real that men wonder: Why all this?" – Then Kapila says: "This reality, the manifested world, is a material world and it is all that we are able to perceive. Its root is in the root-matter, in mūlaprakriti*, whose own essence is mysterious, but which is behind all this existence. Thus all existence is the material manifestation."

Some Europeans reckon Kapila's philosophy to be materialism succeeding Vedanta. But Indians do not believe so. They have a peculiar philosophical system which they call materialism and it is totally different from this. Kapila is not a materialist and is not to be conceived as such. He admits Vedanta being right: This root-substance is the innermost essence of all, but he only explains the emergence of existence, and that is prakriti**, that is real,

---

*Literally 'root-nature'. **Literally 'nature' but used to represent sensible materiality*. (Editor)

that is relative. He emphasizes the relative reality of all phenomenal existence. – Kapila says: "This material reality is not the only one, for what do we perceive? – We perceive it to be of compositional nature, different phenomena of materiality, and none of the parts constituting it exist independently as separate from one another. Let us consider a bed, for example. It has many different parts, but all the parts taken as a whole are called a bed. Does a bed exist for itself? – No, it serves some other purpose. We cannot see anything in nature that would not serve, that would not exist for some other purpose. And from this we come to the conclusion that the compositional entity called man, who is a complex being, also exists for something else than himself. He serves some other purpose."

"What is it that everything serves in this universe? And for what purpose does everything exist? It exists for soul, purusha*, spirit." – And then Kapila presents us a great and wonderful worldview:

"In everything there is purusha, spirit, consciousness that only observes. In reality there is but one purusha, but we know nothing about it until we reach the final end of knowledge. To us there exist multiple purushas. The principle of purusha is behind everything. Behind every form, and especially the human form, there is purusha, spirit that observes. – So what is the relation of purusha and prakriti to each other? They exist alongside each other." – Kapila explains with a metaphor:

"Prakriti is like a healthy and strong man who is blind. Purusha is like a paralyzed, powerless man who has healthy eyes, who sees and sits in the back of this blind man. The blind carries the paralyzes who can see. Prakriti is blind, its nature is that of willing, it must emanate out of itself all kinds of forms and images. Purusha cannot act, it is powerless, it just observes. They are meant for each other,

*Literally 'man', used to represent the principle of consciousness.

(Editor)

or prakriti is meant for purusha, for prakriti displays and purusha observes. The inner essence of prakriti is to display itself to purusha, but it cannot do so properly at once. It shows all kinds of things of itself but purusha does not see immediately. Finally purusha sees."

"Prakriti, materiality, is like a tight-rope walker who presents herself to her audience and lures the eyes of the viewers to herself. And the viewers observe with great interest while the tight-rope walker begins and ends her performance, but they cannot grasp her essence while she is dancing."

"Thus is prakriti to purusha like a young, shy maiden who suddenly notices that her secret was seen, that she was bare to the gaze of man. Then she is terrified and runs away. But when purusha has seen prakriti bare he then knows, and then the connection between purusha and prakriti is loosened, or they become united so that the strong blind man gains sight and the weakness of the paralyzed disappears and there is only one seeing and powerful being."

With such metaphors Kapila describes the relation between purusha and prakriti. And he stays in spiritual matters, in views regarding soul: – "In what way does prakriti appear to purusha? In what form does the tight-rope walker dance before every purusha? – Purusha does not observe the world through our eyes, the task of purusha is to observe its own soul." – And Kapila, agreeing with the Vedanta, says: "Everything is in my consciousness. Nothing would exist if there was not consciousness which is aware of it. Only when there is consciousness there exists that which exists. There would be no existence if there was no consciousness that was aware of it."

When discussing purusha and prakriti Kapila does not mean by prakriti this sensible world: it is a result of the mingling between prakriti and purusha; it is something illusory, secondary, a later derivative. When Kapila discusses prakriti he means the contents of the human purusha, the soul, within which the whole world is included as a secondary phenomenon. All manifestation is prakriti within purusha, the soul. Kapila calls all that appears of prakriti in soul's consciousness as lingam*. – You notice if you are familiar with theosophical vocabulary that it differs from old Indian words, and therefore we must not recall here the theosophical linga sharīra**. However, it is well to note that the theosophical world view and occult views in general are very close in particular to sānkhya.

In Kapila's version, purusha is enveloped in prakriti in the form of lingam. The shape, the type of lingam is the invisible spiritual body of the spirit, purusha, and passes through all the earthly incarnations. Whatever there exists of prakriti in the consciousness of each soul, each particular purusha, manifests through one's lingam which is a kind of individual container of prakriti. Therefore sānkhya studies lingam and its essence.

What is this lingam, how is it formed? – Sānkhya philosophy answers: "Purusha remains always above everything; it is not created and does not create, but lingam is created and creates – just like prakriti. Now prakriti, nature, the essence of materiality, emanates out of itself everything which becomes manifested." – Kapila describes such a view by the name sarga, emanation. What we in the West call creation is from an Indian point of view emanation, or evolution as it is said here in the West. This is what the ancient Indian people said thousands of years ago.

At first prakriti emanates mahat, i.e. buddhi, also called mahābuddhi. Mahā means 'great' and buddhi means 'reason', 'intelligence', but intelligence in a higher meaning so it always includes knowledge. In theosophical literature we use the word buddhi in the context of intuition, seeing truth directly with insight. – So buddhi is intelligence, a world-reason; intelligence that at the same time is knowing and seeing directly and therefore intelligence in a higher sense, consciousness which as intelligence sees directly.

---

*Literally 'a mark', 'a sign'. ** Etheric body. (Editor)

At first it is emanation from prakriti. The next according to Kapila is ahankāra, which means 'I-making', that is, the creating of self; that principle which creates a sense of I.

So at first there is directly seeing pure intelligence, but from it emanates ahankāra, the awareness of self. – "What is the inner essence of this ahankāra?" Kapila asks and goes on to answer: "It is Abhimāna, which means thought with a purpose, thought focused on personal intention of the thinker." – This may sound like an abstruse philosophy. – Mahat, i.e. buddhi is pure reason. Out of that emanates ahankāra, the awareness of self, which always has a purpose.

If we were to describe this in other words we could say that buddhi is pure reason, pure intelligent consciousness which reflects the truth, the real existence, but is like a mirror and has no purpose of its own, it only reflects the surrounding reality as it is. This we call in the theosophical system higher reason. If we say that we utilize higher reason we mean that we have an intelligence which is like a mirror, so that when we turn it on any given point in the universe, it is reflected in that mirror exactly as it is without any distortions. If our higher intelligence is kept clear and pure then it is really a mirror, it reflects no selfishness and sees truth directly. But ahankāra is a different kind of mental process, it is thinking. It is called the lower intellect. It is thinking through an explicit notion of self, it says "I" and then constructs meanings around itself. This ahankāra, the very essence of selfishness, does not see and reflect reality as it is, but views it with regard of personal gain, in what way it could use it for its own benefit.

Such is the lower, calculating intellect of man, which in fact creates our whole culture. It is the calculating intellect which always thinks about itself, and perhaps a few others as well, but always with an intention. And as long as this lower intellect views reality with a biased intent, so long it is unable to see pure truth; its own selfishness clouds the mirror-like clear sight, so that it always reflects distortions, it always corresponds to the person's own desires.

A person colors the truth and twists it in his mind to serve his own opinionated views. And this is all due to ahankāra. The higher intelligence, buddhi, reflects events only in objective light, exactly as they are. In our European way of life ahankāra manifests in a manner that we mentally limit beforehand the world we wish to impartially study. Our scientists state: "We have the truth, there is nothing else, all else is an illusion. If you tell us of ghosts we will laugh at you; the truth is what we perceive with our five senses." – Although there is an intention to unite with buddhi, to objectively see truth as it is, the sly hand of ahankāra is, however, shown in that circle of ignorance it draws. The seeker of truth must therefore beware, let him not give ahankāra any power beforehand, let him set no limits for truth, not close the door of his heart, but let him always be ready to receive truth, being ever more aware that his limitations are enormous.

This fact Kapila points out to us clearly when he discusses buddhi and ahankāra. Next he says: "Only when there is already ahankāra there emanates from it those eleven and five too, so altogether sixteen." – What are those eleven? – They are manas, our ordinary mind, and ten indriyā, literally 'senses', organs of mind. They are divided into a pair: five on the other side and five on the other, and they are in contact with each other through manas. These mental organs are the senses. Five of these indriyā are 'knowledge-senses', buddhi indriyā (buddhīndriyā). But the other five are 'function-organs', karma indriyā*. – What are those first mentioned five knowledge-senses? – They are our senses as we usually know them: sight, hearing, taste, touch and smell. They are the senses our mind, manas, uses for attaining knowledge of the external reality. These organs are all in lingam which is man's soul-body. They are not strictly our physical senses although they are as if reflected into our physical body, for the senses themselves, both of

---

*Written in sanskrit as a compound as karmendriyā (Editor)

knowledge and of action, are in fact in the soul-body, and therefore knowing takes place in it.

What are the five karma indriyā? – They are: vāk, pāda, pānī, pāju and upastha. Vāk is language, voice, the ability to utter sounds, to speak; as a soul-quality it is the ability to give out information regarding oneself through sound, by speaking. Pāda, the feet, are the second functionary organ. Pānī, the hands, are the ability to work, to shape the world. Pāju, the organs for defecation and urination, are as a soul-quality the ability to discharge out of one's system what is redundant. Upastha is the ability to procreate.

These are the functionary organs in the lingam, and they are connected to each other by manas, conscious mind, that willing aspect which makes the organs function. The word manas has a totally different meaning in Kapila's philosophy – and in Indian philosophy in general – than what is has in the theosophical worldview. In theosophical language manas is intellect. So we see that what we usually call in theosophical literature the higher intelligence or reason, is in this system buddhi, and the lower intellect is here ahankāra.

There is an inner consciousness which lies behind all sensations and functions, a unified mind. The Indian philosopher says: "In this body the eye in itself sees nothing, but there is an organ behind the eye which conveys seeing to mind; although the eye receives the images, it is the organ behind it which transmits the obtained image to the consciousness which is behind all these organs, and only then from manas the knowledge of that perception reaches ahankāra and buddhi." – The Indian philosopher is very precise regarding this structure. And the occultist who can follow sensory processes of perception sees that these Indian explanations have a real basis. That is how it all actually happens, although it is presented philosophically.

But Kapila said that besides these eleven, there emanates from the ahankāra other five as well. – What are they? – They are the five tanmātras. If we were to come up with

67

a translation we would say: they are five primary elements, the very essence of those five elements. – With language familiar from the theosophical literature we could say that these five tanmātras are the atomic vibrations of five levels and so also of five elements. The five tanmātras are five different modes of vibration which manifest in five different elements and levels. These primal modes of vibration, atoms as it were or prakriti's possibilities to manifest, exist in the soul-vesture of man, lingam. It is only after appearing in lingam that these five tanmātras form the different sensible elements; and only one of them, sūkshma, stays within lingam, while the other four emanate from it and build up this sensible world. It is said specifically that the four elements outside the lingam are mātā-pitri-jā, born of the parents, 'mother-father-born', which means that they create the world of this coarse body. The whole universe that remains in existence solely by the cosmic procreative force and manifests as coarse matter, appears outside the lingam. And man in lingam travels in this world, and dies, and is born again, but as lingam he is actually outside of this world as it were, transcending it, although he does affect its existence. But his life of illusion in this world of coarse matter created by mother and father lasts only as long as he does not see truth.

VI
REINCARNATION AND THE
PATH OF LIBERATION

As usual in the East, it has been a custom in India to teach the fundamentals of thinking through parables planted within narratives. We have already in these lectures told a few of these Indian tales from the Upanishads, and I would like to share one more from Chandogya. The tale is very descriptive and educative. I mention this in advance, for you will notice several interesting details that are worthwhile to think about.

There was a boy named Shvetaketu. His father, a brahmin priest named Aruni, said to his son when he was twelve years old: "It is now time for you to study the Vedas for there is no one in our family or tribe who has not known the Vedas." – As was customary the boy then left home to join learned Vedic experts. Twelve years he spent in the woods and learned all the Vedas: Rigveda, Yajurveda and Sāmaveda. He learned all the sacred lore. But he became conceited and proud and thought himself to be learned and noble. At the age of twenty four he returned home to his father. Aruni told Shvetaketu: "You have become swollen with pride and think you are learned and noble, my dearest. But have you learned the teaching by which we learn to hear that which cannot be heard, to think what is not thinkable, and to understand the incomprehensible?" – "No, sir," Shvetaketu answered, "I have not heard of that teaching."

– And the father spoke: "As from a clump of clay can be known the essence of all things made of clay, for although all items made of clay are of different shape and name, they are still clay; and likewise can be known all things made of copper – such is this teaching, my dear." "My lord, I have heard nothing of that teaching, my teachers told me nothing of it. If they had known it, why did they not speak anything about it to me? Tell me about it, my lord." And his father Aruni explained:

"The Existent is from whence all has come, the only real being, apart which nothing has ever been. Some claim that in the beginning there was non-existent, but how could non-existent become existent? So at first there was the Existent, and from that Existent everything was born. The Existent said to itself: "I want to multiply and generate." – And it gave birth to heat, or fire. And heat, tejas, said to itself: "I want to multiply and generate." – And it gave birth to water, āpas. And water said to itself: "I want to multiply and generate." – And from itself it gave birth to food, anna. Therefore, my dear, when a human being gives birth in labor to others out of one's self, that fire, tejas in him, generates sweat, water, that secretes out of the person. And when it rains in nature, the result is food emerging from the soil. These three, fire (tejas), water (āpas) and food (anna) all have distinctive densities: the thickest part, the one in the middle and the thinnest part, as it were. When a person eats food (anna) the most solid part goes to waste, the middle one is transformed into flesh and the most subtle into the brain, to memories. When a person takes in water (āpas) the most solid part goes to waste and comes out of the body, the middle one is transformed into blood and the most subtle one is transformed into breath. When a person eats heat (tejas) the most solid part turns to bone, the middle one into marrow and the most subtle one into speech. – Do you wish to hear more, my dearest? –

Just like the most delicate and lightest part of milk rises to the surface and turns to cream, so does the most delicate part of food rise upwards to the head and turn into brains.

70

The most delicate and lightest part of water rises upwards and turns into breath, and the most delicate part of fire turns into speech. – My dearest, do you wish to see this truth? For fifteen days do not eat any food (anna), only drink water as much as you like. Then come to me." –

Shvetaketu fasted for fifteen days drinking only water. Then he came to his father saying: "Here I am now, what would you like me to do? Would you like me to recite something to you?"

– "Yes," said the father, "recite spells from Rigveda, Yajurveda and Sāmaveda." But Shvetaketu was amazed and said: "Oh, my lord, I cannot remember any spells from any of the scriptures." – His father said: "If you have a large pile of coal and of that coal only a portion of the size of a glow-worm is burning it will not affect the large pile, it will not light it up. You have only one of the sixteen parts* functioning properly and your brain cannot remember anything. Eat food, my dearest." – And Shvetaketu ate and then came to his father and said: "Now I remember the spells from Rigveda, Yajurveda and Sāmaveda." The father said: "Yes my dearest, if there is a large pile of coal and of that only a portion of the size of a glow-worm is burning it will not affect the large pile, it will not light it up, but if you place any of the food stuffs on it, like dry hay, it will catch fire." – "My lord, what do you wish for me to do now?" – "My dearest, take a fig and halve it." – "I have done so, my lord." – "What do you see in it?" – "I see a seed." – "Take the seed and halve it." – "I have done so, my lord." – "What do you see?" – "I no longer see anything." – "My dearest, in that seed which is so small that when you split it in half there is nothing inside, there still is the force of a great fig tree to grow. Through that force the tiny seed

---

* Man is made of sixteen parts which are composed of the three basic elements, fire, food and water. But now after fasting for fifteen days your body has only one of its sixteen parts functioning properly, and that is because you still kept drinking water although you did not take food. (Editor)

becomes a great tree. Likewise is He, God, present everywhere, even where you do not see Him. Seek the Self which abides with God, seek that, my dearest, and you will attain knowledge."

That whole story was rich in content. It naturally fits very well to Vedanta and the Upanishads, but there are also points which clearly surpass also Kapila's sānkhya philosophy, of which we wish to continue a little more. The interesting part in that story for those studying sānkhya philosophy is the trinity, for the story clearly talks about that which becomes manifested, of prakriti, nature, which in itself in not manifested but out of which emerges all that what becomes manifested.

Sānkhya philosophy emphasizes the fact that the essence of nature is three-fold, it has three different aspects. It does not use the names just discussed: fire, water and food, but it uses different, more descriptive and philosophical terms. These names are familiar to all, they are the gunas.

There are tree modes in the manifested nature, prakriti. – What do they signify? – They are the three gunas: sattva, rajas, and tamas; of these tamas is between and below sattva and rajas. Sattva means pleasantness, preference. Literally it has a different meaning and when modified it means many things: light, lightness, peacefulness and so forth, but here it means preference. Rajas means aversion and tamas indifference.

Sānkhya philosophy explains that in manifested nature, within materiality, there are three basic modes, or qualities: pleasantness, aversion and indifference. It is the fundamental essence of all manifestation. In sānkhya philosophy it is said that if in any object or being has, in relation to us, the quality of sattva, it will generate pleasantness. Rajas generates aversion in us, and if there is tamas it will have no effect on us, it leaves us indifferent. These basic qualities in all manifestations mix together, so that one and the same quality may manifest different qualities in us and different in other living beings. This depends on the living being himself and the world surrounding him.

Let us say we have a friend. He can then, relating to us, manifest the qualities of sattva, rajas or tamas. First he has manifested qualities of sattva, he has been our friend. Then he manifests the qualities of rajas, and he no longer is our friend – he brings about pain and suffering in us. But after a while we overcome the pain and suffering and then the quality of tamas surfaces and he becomes meaningless to us.

But the same object, or being, may at the same time manifest different qualities. When players play from money the same pile of money affects everyone present differently. To the winner it gives out sattva-quality, it evokes pleasantness in him, but for the one who loses it has the rajas-aspect, feelings of hate and bitterness, while a third person, watching the game, remains indifferent about the money. – At the same time the same pile of gold has different effect according to the conscious beings. The pile of gold contains in it different qualities, it contains these three factors.

Now of course those familiar with theosophical literature remember that these basic qualities, sattva, rajas, and tamas, are also used as descriptive names – at least sometimes – for different planes. It is said that the physical plane has as its basic quality tamas, the astral plane has rajas and the mental plane has sattva. That is not exactly accurate for these qualities are everywhere, but there is some truth in it. Realistically it is true that the sattva-quality is most dominant in the mental word, rajas in the astral world and tamas in the physical.

This is spoken of also in sānkhya philosophy, for after all it lays specific emphasis on the threefold mode of nature. It is said that food, anna, is threefold, as is fire and water, all three containing three levels of densities, totaling altogether nine different densities. If we examine this we notice that in the coarsest food types there are most qualities of tamas, in the middle there are most qualities of rajas and in the most subtle, the qualities of sattva, which rise upwards and form the brain. We also notice that sānkhya philosophy uses these names and teaches that they correspond with the manifestations of matter, because sānkhya speaks of three worlds of different density, and it is especially said that the subtlest one, sūkshma, is the one closest to the original state of prakriti, meaning here buddhi. Sūkshma is the only one which stays after death in lingam, in soul's vesture: the other two do not, they always dissolve.

Now when we adopt the view of sānkhya philosophy we remember that purusha, spirit, consciousness, the self, is beyond the nature, the observer outside of it, as it were. We remember the parable of the paralyzed man sitting in the back of the blind man. Purusha only observes but is attached to prakriti, matter; it does not create, does not bring about anything. Prakriti is the one that creates everything. Nature forms everything, so that from nature there emanates buddhi, the subtlest and highest aspect of truth.

It is said in sānkhya philosophy that purusha is always united with lingam, the soul-body, the immutable body. Purusha is always united to that, but is born on Earth multiple times. Indian philosophy in all its different forms, in its six orthodox schools, always agrees that man is a reincarnating being. The spirit of a man is not clad for the first time in its vesture, lingam, but has been here before and shall again be. From the Indian viewpoint of reincarnation, purusha, spirit, is tied to samsāra, or the cycle of birth and death in matter, before it is liberated. Liberation is salvation from the chains of prakriti. Purusha, being the observer, is not really tied to anything; prakriti is chained and the liberation occurs when purusha sees the secret of prakriti. But because spirit is always above all matter, matter itself is chained and tied to itself and dependent on spirit until it has been able to reveal its secret to the spirit, like the young girl bathing in the parable. Then prakriti is freed from its own chains. And because this does not happen to all people in their lives, because it is obvious that most people are not liberated during their life time and because there are few who are liberated, whose spirit sees the secret of all nature, and a mutual liberation for purusha as well as prakriti occurs, the Indian philosophy reasons that there must be rebirth.

Sānkhya philosophy says that over and over again matter gives spirit a chance to see the secret of matter. Matter repeatedly gives spirit a chance. It is like the tightrope walker who always does tricks and lures, but reveals no secret and no one really sees her properly. Over and over again she acts the same way. This is exactly the relation between prakriti and purusha. Over and over again nature dances before spirit and asks: "Do you yet see who I am? I wish you would, so that I could become free." Such is the eternal prayer of matter.

But lingam is the material vesture which is joined to the spirit, always similar, immutable. And we ask: "Why then are people different when their spirit is always dressed in same materiality? – What constitutes the differences of men?" Sānkhya philosophy answers: All differences are due to bhāvas. Bhāvas are the innate qualities and results which are attached to each purusha and he's lingam in the births. – So what are these bhāvas? – Bhāva means a state of being, and also something like suffering. It could be thought of in comparison to the Greek word pathé, which means pain, suffering, sickness. The word pathology is derives from it. So in a sense the teaching of these bhāvas is a teaching of the sicknesses of the lingam, as we have medicine researching the pathological states of the varying constitutions of human physical body. So the bhāvas are in a sense the sicknesses hidden in the lingam of the human purusha and they generate the differences between men.

What causes bhāvas? – They are generated by the three modes of prakriti: sattva, rajas and tamas. They mingle together in various ways and have different effects. And when we take into account that it is really a question of three different worlds, planes in which all these three gunas produce effects and mingle together, then we understand how in men there are born so many different and varying effects and manifestations.

It is said that in buddhi, the first and highest emanation of prakriti, there are four bhāvas, four basic "diseases", as it were, but in fact when thought of like this, they are four basic conditions of health, with diseases hiding under the surface of each and producing the individual characteristics of each basic "health". The four bhāvas in buddhi are: dharma, vairāgya, aishvarya and jñāna. Dharma means religiousness, lawfulness, the fulfillment of salvation. It is a word of many meanings. Madame Blavatsky chose as the maxim of the Theosophical Society the phrase: "Satyān nāsti paro dharmah", which means: "There is no dharma, religion, higher than truth". – Every person's dharma is one's destined life-purpose, and it varies with every person. Therefore the Bhagavad Gita says: "There is nothing as dangerous as trying to accomplish someone else's dharma. Let everyone deal with their own dharma and leave the other's be." – All that is contained in the word dharma. This is the basic condition of health in buddhi. Its opposite is adharma, atheism, being ignorant of one's dharma, unlawfulness.

The second bhāva in buddhi is vairāgya: it means desirelessness, denial, almost asceticism; the refusal from all kinds of pleasures, of all that are not in accord with God's will. That is one of the basic lines of buddhi. Therein lies the seed to the disease avairāgya, which is desire for sensual pleasures and contempt towards all abstinence.

The third is aishvarya, which means lordship, godliness, control of oneself, total power over oneself, so that such a being can be called a master, a god. The opposite of this is anaishvarya, which means inability to control oneself, being a slave to one's lower Self.

The fourth is jñāna, knowledge, which is a basic quality of buddhi. Buddhi is the possibility to see truth. When purusha sees the secret of matter, it happens with the help of buddhi, and that is jñāna. It is hidden in buddhi but its opposite is also hidden as a possibility, and it is called ajñāna, ignorance.

These things become clear to us when we think about them in relation to the tripleworld, triloka, and above it the real spiritual world. The three planes of the tripleworld are the physical, astral and mental planes, or the planes of action, feeling and intellect.

Above the mental plane of intellect begins the plane of spirit. When we think of man's lingam, and buddhi as its first and highest emanation, we have the three worlds, the three planes. Now the bhāvas correspond best to these planes, so that on the physical plane we have dharma and adharma, on the astral plane vairāgya and avairāgya, on the mental plane of intellect we have aishvarya and anaishvarya, and on the level of spirit jñāna and ajñāna.

When we look at a man's life from the point of view of sānkhya philosophy we see as follows:

A man lives in this visible, physical world and it is his duty to hear the voice of dharma. If he does not hear and obey dharma he hears adharma. Here dharma represents religion, law, order of life and thus the sacred duty of every person's life. So a person should be loyal to dharma, he should be religious, obey the law and find out about his own moral duty in life. If he lives as nature intends him to live he will adapt to the rule of life and strives to obey dharma. But if he is not a thinking and striving person he will be under the influence of adharma. This will affect reincarnation. His own way of life, his choices here, depend on the mixtures in his being. If there is a lot of tamas, darkness or heaviness and ignorance in him, he will live as if in a dream, he does not think much, is not a person who tries to accomplish or create something, but in a dream-like state just lives by going with the flow. Then he may out of ignorance obey religions and laws, but may just as well do the opposite. His life in the physical world affects his reincarnation. If he follows dharma, obeys the rules of religion and so forth, then this will affect his reincarnation in the way that when he will be born again he will be born to better conditions.

If he lives in adharma his next birth will be into worse conditions.

Then on the emotional level there are vairāgya and avairāgya. On the astral plane, if a person is spiritually striving upwards, he will be abstaining in his emotional life. If he obeys the voice of life astrally, if he obeys the voice of nature and spirit in regard to his desires, he will abstain from indulging himself. But if he does not do so, he throws himself at the mercy of his wants and desires. This will also affect reincarnation. Sānkhya philosophy explains that it affects reincarnation in a way that if a person abstains, then prakriti will be formed for him of lighter density, his prakriti in will not gather heaviness, tamas. He will get a body which is light and of which dense materiality diminishes. On the contrary, if he does not abstain, he will become more coarse, more a slave of reincarnation. There is something in his being which weighs on him and drags him downwards.

Then we have aishvarya and anaishvarya. Aishvarya is having mastery over oneself, and anaishvarya is the lack of that. If a person lives according to the voice of life he will strive to become a master, he wishes not to be a slave to himself, he does not wish to be like a servant in the house but a lord of the house, a master in his own body. This is striving towards aishvarya. – What is the result of this? It follows that nature obeys his wishes: his wishes become fulfilled. Life obeys him because he is a master over himself, and nature serves him. His wishes are unselfish, they are not directed towards himself, they are of divine quality and therefore they are fulfilled. On the other hand if a person does not strive for aishvarya but is caught in anaishvarya and becomes a slave to his lower nature, then that will affect his reincarnation in a way that nature will not serve him, but will resist him. His wishes will not come true, they are in vain for life puts obstacles in his way.

Jñāna and ajñāna correspond to the world of spirit, the world of higher reason, higher manas. Actually ajñāna covers all the others beneath it, so there are in total seven forms of ignorance. The only thing that can liberate is jñāna. It is not yet enough that a person lives out dharma, vairāgya and aishvarya; he must rise above all that. Everything is ignorance in relation to true jñāna. Knowledge is the highest that will redeem.

As we see sānkhya philosophy teaches of karma: it does not emphasize what we in the West call free will. Sānkhya teaches that the basic elements of nature are within man, they struggle together and cause effects. Man reincarnates until he finally wakes into knowledge. But one should not make a conclusion from this that Indian philosophy would not consider free will a reality. On the contrary, sānkhya explicitly expounds that a man must strive to gain the eight perfections, the eight siddhis. And he will face many obstacles. One obstacle is a belief that nature will in the end take man to salvation. There are even theosophists in our days who say that nature will take man by karma and reincarnation to salvation, and man cannot do anything himself. Sānkhya philosophy says that this is erroneous and we must get rid of the idea. A man must strive and aspire himself or nothing will be accomplished. – All Indian philosophies speak of yoga, and there naturally is yoga in sānkhya philosophy, but because this path of yoga is of such importance, in India they have made it into a system of yoga, to which philosophers refer to.

Liberation is reached when the spirit of man, purusha, sees the secret of matter. But in what way we can strive for liberation and of what kind of karma we must be free of – this yoga tells us.

VII
THE YOGA MEDITATION OF PATANJALI

When we talk about the East and the West in a spiritual sense we do not mean any geographical areas with these words; with the East we mean the time and accomplishments before Jesus Christ, and with the West we mean the time and accomplishments after Jesus Christ. But we do not call these things for example "the pagan world" and "Christendom", for Christendom is not yet a true Christendom. The so-called Christendom is still young; it has not yet developed into any real Christendom nor has it gained any triumphs of Christ, whereas the pagan world, or the Eastern lands are so old that they have had the time to become what they are. They have really shown, and still show what they have been able to accomplish before Jesus Christ.

In a spiritual sense we make this distinction between the East and the West. – If we wanted to briefly describe the different spirit of the East and the West – we talk of the spirit of the West even though it is still young – when again the spirit of the East is, so to say, the spirit of a child or a youth when we think of the ancient past. Now we talk about the old East, which is like a wise old man, but if we go far back in time its spirit is like that of a child and a youth; it is joyous faith in that man's purpose is to find truth and God. One who is of Eastern spirit understands that his task is to seek and find God.

But the Western spirit is a bit different. After Jesus Christ it is as if we all had already seen God. We cannot say it is so in our everyday mind, but deep within every man who has heard of Jesus Christ, whether this man lives in the East or the West, has seen God in the sense that he certainly knows within what a divine human is like, what God on earth is like. Jesus Christ has shown this in a mysterious way; everybody knows this. We cannot debate about it, but we know it.

A Westerner thinks: "How can I, being so lowly and sinful, seek God, truth, and find truth in spiritual way? How can I, who am so imperfect, become one with God? How could God manifest through me?" – This is the mood of a Western man's soul. – And yet this is exactly the same as the Eastern mood. In the West this is already the beginnings of seeking truth. This Western mood regards more to our will, the Eastern regards more to our thought. We did not know about the reality of perfection until Jesus Christ showed it. In the East Buddha was as perfect, Lao Tzu in China, Zoroaster in Persia, and other liberators as well, but they were not God on earth in all totality as was Jesus Christ. However they were all full of still are all filled with life's brightness. Therefore they said: "Follow me and you shall find truth." But Jesus Christ was like a ripe fruit, that is perfect in every sense from since a childhood. Therefore he showed us something that cannot vanish from our souls. It is such information which shows us that we are all imperfect.

These two are however the same thing for man is called upon to seek truth and God, and to find them. Here in the West many have found them, but the majority of people have not even tried to seek. We have not even wanted to know that we should try, but we have lulled ourselves into the idea that we cannot do anything. We seek such a view on life that we can trust on the success of others. We forgot to try; we forgot that life is a path. And this forgetfulness is the cause why the Eastern yoga seems unfamiliar to us. When it is said that yoga is the means through which man gains knowledge of the most profound secret of himself and life, of life and death, then a Christian thinks: "What childishness is this? This is of Indian heritage; they have fakirs who do all kinds of tricks. They do not have Christ, therefore they have those tricks, but we have Christ." – A Christian thinks that yoga is unnecessary. But yoga is necessary to everyone who wishes to seek and find God, for yoga is the way to a union with God.

The first steps of Indian yoga are lessons of morality, the next are exoteric in the sense that in the yogic procedures of man they deal more with his body, his senses and outer personality. But the three last steps are, like Patanjali says, esoteric compared to the others for they deal only with man's soul, *chitta*, the principle of intellect, the intellect-body. It is this very thinking that has been totally forgotten in Christianity, although it was of course known in the beginning. Therefore Christianity has stopped with its first achievement: the knowing of one's own inferiority. But stopping there is very dangerous. And that which alone can save Christianity from this state it has gotten into is yoga meditation. Moral requirements are understood but their necessity is not always understood. Meditation, prayer, is not known in the meaning Jesus Christ used it.

This meditation, when we want to study it according to Patanjali, has as its first step concentration, which is called dhāranā in Sanskrit. Patanjali says of this first step: fixing the chitta in one target is dhāranā. Dhāranā itself means bearing, or holding. If we ask what this concentration is, we are required of being aware of all terms and requirements Patanjali has spoken of, which one must fulfil before he can begin to meditate. He must be of moral quality. – Then he must have a posture which does not disturb him, so that his attention is easily drawn away from the surrounding world. – And also he must have learned to breathe calmly. Many people have a tendency to breathe too fast. All this is exercised before actual yoga takes place. One sits down in a comfortable posture which enables his soul as well to take a kind of calm "posture". Then he practices concentration, he fixes his chitta, his intelligence-principle to one target. He

83

takes control of his soul, i.e. intellect-body, sort of like "takes it in his hand" and holds it in one place. – Let us remember here what the great Protestant teacher Luther, says: "The intellect must be caught and thrown under the chair. The intellect is too stubborn to understand divine truth." – This is of course a dangerous sentence if we understand that we must not seek truth with our reason. This might have been so in Luther's time, but it would be folly to understand this so that we should not seek truth, to get to know all religions, philosophies and sciences as much as is humanly possible. On the contrary, we must develop our reason as much as possible. But this is one of those things that precede yoga. These days we are not likely to begin practicing yoga unless we are at least somewhat sensible and intelligent.

So this Luther's sentence is not suitable in a too early stage, but strangely enough it arises in yoga. As humans we must make this observation that our reason and understanding will not help us see the innermost truth; we will not find God with our reason. The quality of reasoning is that it measures and evaluates, but God is beyond all measurements. Our reason is always assessing, but God cannot be assessed. If we wish to find God, the Truth and study yoga with this aim in mind, we will then come to the point that we must learn to meditate, we must understand that the reason must surrender obediently. In front of the divine majesty all it asks is: "Help me see!" –

Then the first exercise is that man takes control of his mind – for a long time, years, every day, he "takes his mind by the hand". It is something he must experience. Thought is pinned in one place so that the thought-body is still. Then the thought-body is at peace; in other words it is still in extremely rapid vibration but it is at peace. All permutations, which Patanjali described the "births and deaths", happen so fast that it is peace. When a man practices concentration he takes for example a pencil and studies it at first. Then he closes his eyes and tries to see this pencil in his consciousness, with his "soul's eyes". – Then he notices what a wild colt his mind is. All kinds of other thoughts and pictures come along, which disturb him so that he cannot always see this pencil. All kinds of thoughts come to mind, and he questions himself: "What are you, sensible person fooling about?" – One notices that he has no control over his mind. This is the first very healthy observation. When a person has practiced this, for example, seven years and has gradually progressed from being a slave to his mind, to the point where he already has a slight control of his mind, then he understands it is supposed to be so, for what is he as a spiritual being if he does not control his own house? He is a slave in his own house who does what is told. But when a man, a yogi has gained some control over his mind he is no longer a slave, but a son in the house. This achievement is not totally impossible for there are people who have practiced it in their previous lives and are now born with this skill. All sages, geniuses, creative people have this ability to some extent, although there are many sorts of concentration. There is an easy way too, but true concentration is difficult. – I can concentrate my thoughts if I want to, say, carve a spoon. I cannot carve it if I do not think about it. This is easy concentration that life teaches to everyone. Everybody who perform their daily tasks properly in life can concentrate a little, but concentration becomes hard if we do not act in the physical world, but retreat to inaction, into spirit, away from this visible world. Then we are in a different field and notice that we cannot concentrate.

Dhāranā is spiritual work. It is conquering thought. And when one is slightly progressed in this, Patanjali says that he then develops in him that which is called *nirodha parināma,* which means literally the modification of restraint. Patanjali says that this follows the practice of dhāranā. These words can also be translated otherwise. *Parinama* also means destination. Then we can extract from those words what experience proves, that when such concentration, dhārana, happens in a specific time of meditation, it follows that this restraint, prevention of movements in the mind becomes easier every day, from which follows a steady motion, a stream. This means that a person practicing dhāranā will attain a peaceful mind. Although his mind is not concentrated otherwise than that specific time, it still affects so that at the next time of meditation the concentration is easier and his mind is calm all along the day. He of course carries out all his duties – everyone has their duties in the outer life and his task as a yogi is to fulfil all his duties as well as possible. This is all possible because he becomes serene. If we look for a predominant quality in men, it is the restlessness of the mind, its tendency to flare up. Man lives so deep in his emotions that all things make him restless; all kinds of events and things in life disturb him. But when he learns to meditate he will then attain peace of mind; nothing will stir him anymore.

Patanjali says that the next step is dhyāna, meditation proper. He describes dhyāna, translated literally, as follows: dhyāna follows this concentration of mind onto one subject. – Usually meditation means that a person learns to keep his thoughts in one place, he chooses a subject and thinks about it. For example he chooses a question: What is truth, goodness? – and thinks, meditates it from different angles.

I think that a small error is made herein. It is thought that it is meditation when one thinks about a pencil, for example. Even one teacher of the occult arts in our time has said that thinking about an object can be called a meditation. That is a mistake, for that is just concentration, dhāranā. You cannot concentrate thought on emptiness; one must have something to concentrate on. It is not meditation in a sense Patanjali means.

We can translate this sentence of Patanjali´s in a different way. The Sanskrit word *pradhaya* means not only attention but also conviction, faith, which is its original meaning. The Europeans have had to add other meanings, for they would not have understood these words. In the West we have used the Latin word meditation and given it the meaning we have. But in reality the word means piety. Meditation i.e. dhyāna must be understood as such: the concentration of faith into one subject is followed by piety. – We do not understand this straight away, but one with experience knows this. It means that one cannot move from dhāranā to meditation, i.e. dhyāna without faith having been born in him; this mystical thing that is so difficult to define. It is daring, faith, action. The will of man has also had to have awoken.

When we say that the East is better described by thought and the West by will, it is really so. The working of intellect and thought is very intact in the East, but in the West man is troubled with the difficulties in willing: "I am so flawed." – But in the East we are faced with the question of faith, will. It is the system of Patanjali. In yoga faith is in a latter phase. From dhāranā, the mechanical concentration of thought, we must move on to dhyāna, and this happens with the aid of faith. When man has gained faith, when his divine will has come alive, then can he practice dhyāna i.e. piety. Then his meditation becomes fruitful.

Once in my youth when I was abroad, an old theosophist confessed to me: "I have been an esoterist for 18 years but I do not get any results, I have made no observations." I was only very young then; I did not know to ask what he had done, for they were secret matters, but we had a little chat. I could not discern like I can now, but I did make the observation that his meditation was unfruitful and dry because he had carried on concentration without gaining faith. Faith must awaken in man; then he can fruitfully meditate upon something. When man for example meditates upon "what is goodness", then feeling of piety enters him; it is as if his soul was elevated. When he cannot meditate he says: "Now I just concentrate my thoughts; I cannot meditate now." – Meditation is piety coming from faith; man sees this goodness, its manifestations.

Then Patanjali adds that from dhyāna follows *Samādhi parināma,* which translated literally means trance modification or trance destination. Patanjali explains: when the nature of chitta, the thought-principle has evolved into human mind it concentrates its attention to everything.

87

– In the West we say: "When we have developed ourselves as self-aware humans then our senses have become keen". – In chitta is the ability to focus on thousands of things. But when one practices dhyāna this chitta's "concentration on everything" becomes "concentration on one thing." The word *ekāgratā* in the text means "one-peaked". It means that when one has made real progress in dhyāna he nears samādhi. Then his meditation during the day is ekāgratā, directed at one point. Then he can during the day think about and know God. He is no longer limited to think about God only during his time of meditation, but he can fulfil his everyday duties whilst being in the divine life with his whole attention. All else in his life is like a shadowy image although he can and is able to perform all his tasks perfectly. – This is a profound secret or step in the spiritual life. For the third step is samādhi. That is translated with the Latin word contemplation. Of it Patanjali says (translated literally): "And this, when it just shines the light of the object and is as if free of its own body is samādhi." – This is a very complex, while also an excellent depiction. When dhyāna, meditation is free of chitta, man's own thought-principle, and only shines with the light of the object, then it is samādhi. This means: when meditating on something, for example "what is goodness", one goes past this ordinary stage of meditation, and is completely liberated from chitta as an instrument; he freed from being a thinking and discerning entity and only shines with the light of this goodness in his thought-body. We can say that goodness is like the sun. When we start to meditate, our chitta, thought-principle is an egg-shaped light phenomenon filled with all hues of colour. Then we quiet everything down: the chitta turns white. Then if we meditate and from this light of the chitta look upon the sun of goodness we see in it wondrous things. But when we forget the light of our own chitta and let that sun touch it our own light becomes transformed, becomes that sun, and we are in that sun, in goodness; we are this goodness. Then we undoubtedly know best what goodness is, if there is such a thing in itself.

In meditation we can create our own images and also look at truth, but if it turns into samādhi it turns into truth; nothing but truth can withstand in it. If we have decided for example to study goodness in samādhi we will find out if there really is such a thing, or is it just in our imagination. If it does exist it will enter us. The Easterners say that with yoga one can reach truth; yoga is used to study what is the truth.

When samādhi is practiced then it develops into a new parināma, and this is very peculiar. This is *ekāgratā parināma,* which means that when one practices samādhi he will all day long possess all the habits and customs which emanate from dhāranā and dhyāna and samādhi.

When one practices all of these three kinds of meditation Patanjali says he has then gained control over himself. Samdhyāna is the achievement of yoga; it follows that a visibility of knowledge is born. For example when one is skilled in samdhyāna then all knowledge first from the invisible world and next from the visible world are visible to him. – Only after this Patanjali continues to describe what results yoga provides, what abilities man can attain with yoga.

VIII
THE ATTAINMENTS OF A YOGI

When a yogi has learned the art of concentration he will know it from the fact that the concentration of his thoughts becomes easier every time he meditates, and all along the day in all of his actions he remains especially calm.

When a yogi has learned the art of meditation, dhyāna, he will know it from the fact that his mind which used to be scattered on all things all day long, like Patanjali says, is now learning while making observations to keep its thoughts always focused on one thing, like God, the truth, for example. So he can be in the middle of dutifully filling his tasks and still be focused all day long on the object of his meditation, which is his faith in God. And he will learn to meditate only when he has learned the secret of faith.

When a yogi then learns samādhi, the art of contemplation, or inner sight, then will he have the special ability to always quickly and easily *see* internally what he thinks. His capability for knowledge has mysteriously advanced, broadened.

When a yogi has learned these three skills he will have learned *samdhyāna*, which is the highest achievement of a yogi's meditation. A yogi who has learned to meditate does it by resorting to samdhyāna.

These three processes themselves bring about different

91

alterations in the yogi's constitution. Patanjali does not describe them precisely; he merely states that they happen in dharma, lakshana and avasthā. *Dharma* means here basic quality, *lakshana* means quality in another state and *avasthā* means a random state.

The explanation of this first subject I think comes from the word dharma, which means responsibility, especially religious task. It is common to call religion and religious doctrine dharma. This dharma is the task of man which is given to him naturally in this particular reincarnation. But when we go to India and ask how do they understand the word, they reply that it is their religion; and every religion has its own dharma. – Is it then a religious doctrine? – That is how it is commonly understood in the West. When we have different views on life we argue and even wage wars against each other. In India there are hundreds of different sects and religions and they never argue about such religious doctrines. Why not? – It is because they understand all things differently. They understand that all people naturally have their own thoughts and opinions about the matters of faith and God. All sects have their own understanding of God; it is a thing which belongs to tolerance. For them religion is what a man is supposed to do. In this sense the Orientals are conservative. They think that religion is in actions, ceremonies and rituals. This is their religion; it is clearly a doctrine of morality. Therefore if they would argue it would be due to their religious ceremonies and dharma would being so differing that they would become upset toward each other – but even this is not common.

To this sentence about yoga we get an explanation from the oriental view that the core of religion is always in the actions. When we understand that dharma means action we ask straight away what causes the responsibilities of man in each life. This is not the same as karma. Karma is that which faces man; he is born to the surroundings and circumstances as they are in his karma, and this also includes that which he faces from outward circumstances. But dharma is within the field of one's liberty; what he must do in life that he would advance morally.

On what does dharma depend? –

When we study man occultly we notice that his dharma depends on his body – both physical and etheric. In his physical body are his basic qualities, those tendencies, deeply rooted habits and characteristic traits one cannot change. – Astrologically it is said that one's character is one's destiny. One cannot alter his character. Lao Tzu says: "If someone comes to me telling that someone has changed into a totally different man of character then I would say it is not possible because one cannot change his character". – This is his dharma, from there it starts. As is my character, such is my basis. When there are flaws in my character they are such that I have to turn into assets. But how is this possible? Usually this is not possible, for experience tells us that one rarely can change his inborn nature.

Yoga, on the other hand insists that changes happen in dharma, lakshana and avasthā. Lakshanas are qualities, or states of the astral body and avasthā s are in the higher, i.e. mental body. Our whole life is partly random moods, partly resonating undercurrents prevalent in our emotional body. We have accustomed ourselves to feelings that are dear to us, but besides that we have the ability to have random states of mind.

The practice of yoga results in a change. The random moods cease to exist in a sense that they would be his moods. He has no longer any kinds of moods. The lakshanas, or feelings, all kinds of attractive and repulsive, cease to exist in a sense that they would be the yogi's own moods. And when this has happened a third transformation regarding dharma starts taking place in: the tendencies of his character begin to gradually change. The effects travel through the astral body all the way to the physical body, in which physiological changes can happen. – We cannot discuss more about this here, but this is a subject to meditate upon.

When we understand this aphorism we also understand the next subtle warning of Patanjali's wherein he says that this meditation of a yogi, samādhāna, progresses from level to level. He says: "The order must be followed, otherwise the results are uncertain." – We understand well both of these aphorisms. It is the order and progression from level to level which is vital here, for at first one must purify his thoughts, then the emotions will be purified, which will in the end start to affect the physical body.

Then Patanjali moves on to discuss the attainments which a yogi can attain with his own efforts and with the help of samādhāna by wanting exactly those attainments. They are attained almost without effort by just knowing in which order to practice yoga. A yogi chooses a subject and says he will meditate upon that. Now follows in the sūtras of Patanjali a lengthy listing of attainments. It is of tremendous value because it clearly states what a yogi must meditate, upon what to focus his samādhāna to be able to attain this or that specific thing.

At first Patanjali says: "If a yogi practices samādhāna regarding dharma, lakshana and avasthā, meditates changes in his organism he will then gain knowledge of both the future and the past." – We can add: this knowledge deals with the matters of this incarnation. We note how Patanjali is scientific in his technique of yoga. All such results are achieved in a natural way. When one meditates on these changes which take place in his different vehicles he is able to see how it happens. He meditates upon a temporary state of mind; he notices how it is caused and where it will lead, and from there on how it will vanish and die. When he has determined its whole birth he will then examine what causes the fact that these states can so easily be born. And when he examines the emotional body he sees from what particular emotional basis it is born of; he sees what has originally caused it and where it will lead. Thus he comes to find which of his characteristics this mood is dependent of. Then he observes it and finds out whether that trait is very fixed or loose: from that he can reckon how long he should meditate on it to be able to change it. This sounds complex and mysterious. – A yogi once said to me: "If I randomly make the observation that I have a certain deficiency in my character, I retreat to meditation and with samādhāna I have in 20 minutes in deep meditation removed that deficiency from myself."

Then Patanjali says: "A yogi can use samādhāna for samskāras." – Samskāras are the same as skandhas, the seeds which we bring with us from the past life, our tendencies for good and evil – which are in our physical-etheric organism. All these seeds or samskāras are such that a yogi can practice samdhyāna on them. And when he meditates upon them he can then gain knowledge of his previous incarnations. In this context Patanjali discusses a little about karma, for these samskāras are karmic, brought by karma. Patanjali says: "There are two kinds of karma, and both must be studied by the yogi." – For karma is either fast or slow; it can actualize quickly or slowly. So those seeds develop and bear fruit quickly or slowly.

The most ancient commentator, interpreter, takes two metaphors from nature of how we might understand the quickness and slowness of karma. He says: "If a cloth is very wet it will dry soon if it is spread out properly, but slowly if it is in a bundle. If on the other hand there is a large amount of dry hay in a pile they will burn quickly, the wind benefitting. But what a task fire has if we spread the hay all over the ground!" – So water and fire work totally differently. It is as if he had wanted to tell us with these examples that one should not cling to forms. Karma can be dismantled quickly by spreading out or by gathering, collecting – and vice versa slowly. It depends on the nature of samskāras.

So when meditating on these samskāras in himself one must find out how this specific karma can affect him. Then he shall notice from where it was born. He must take these into account to be able to see whether it has been born either from good or evil.

When a yogi meditates on karma he will, while gaining knowledge of his previous birth, also gain knowledge of the length of this life. A yogi can know when he will die. This of course is a very strange attainment. Peculiar enough the commentators add: "If a yogi cannot find out about this with his own meditations he can tell it from the portents." He receives strange portents of three kinds. The first of these is such – we must notice that this only concerns a yogi – that when a yogi covers his ears he cannot hear the sound of his own body, the flow of blood. This predicts that he will die soon. – Another portent is that when he presses his eyes he does not see the light of the eye; then he will soon die. – The third of the portents is that unexpectedly the yogi is visited by messengers from the realm of death, most likely his own relatives, and this predicts the yogi's death. – This last topic does not have to mean that to us regular people.

This kind of magical ideas exist in great amounts among different peoples and some of them have originated from occult circles, so they have meant a great deal to a yogi, but they need not be any portents to other people.

These divine portents are such that the yogi unexpectedly sees gods and divine worlds, or such that what he sees around him changes into something he has never seen in all his life. For example he will see heaven on earth and see men as gods. Then also is his death imminent.

I can add as an example here that I know a case when a person saw heaven on earth. He was not a yogi so to him it did not mean death.

The next attainment according to Patanjali is: "When a yogi meditates on the image, knowledge, feeling he has of another person, then this person's chitta enters his view and he will get to know his thought and emotional auras. This does not mean that he would know what this person thinks in his chitta." – Using theosophical terms we say: if a yogi meditates on the information he has of another person he can see his aura, but not what he is currently thinking; a yogi can see from another person's aura that he is, for example, in love, but he cannot see to whom. This the commentator specifically adds.

Then Patanjali discusses many other attainments. A yogi can learn the language of all living creatures. – In what way? In such a way that he meditates, practices samdhyāna, on the differences of the word, the object and the idea. In everyday life the word, the object and the idea are one, the commentator states. I will try to explain what is meant by this.

When we speak the word "table", what happens to us that we all know? – Firstly: the word "table" is carried to our ear with airwaves, but it is not just this word but with it the image of the object enters our consciousness. – But the image might vary; not everyone gets the same image of a table; one might see a three-legged one, one a four-legged one, and another a dining table or a writing desk etc. Everyone will get some kind of an image in their mind. Because there are so many images of a table, this has ordinarily comprised two sides of the matter: the word and the object, but not the idea. This does not come to mind. – What is the idea of a table? – It is some kind of a board standing on legs and is not used for sitting, it is used for placing tools or food on it. The idea of a table as an abstract concept exists. And for example Plato says: "Thoughts, ideas are realities. All phenomena in this visible world is but an illusion, images and reflections of ideas; but an idea is eternal." This is true. All tables can vanish, but the idea of a table does not. New tables can always be made when an idea exists.

So these three things exist: word, object and idea. Upon these a yogi must meditate, practice samdhyāna upon these so that he may get from the word and the object to the idea. When he grasps the idea he will understand all languages. This is very true. Let us think that we had the knowledge of what is the idea of a table in the invisible world of pure reason as a concrete phenomenon. What would follow? – It follows that if we hear someone talking about a table in whatever language, this touches upon the idea. And even if we do not see the image in his mind, his voice, his word has with his imagination touched upon the idea so we see this

97

idea as well. How else would extremely luminous beings know of the thoughts of men? Exactly so that everything what we do and talk here is somehow reflected in the world of ideas. It is just as if we played an instrument here and it would sound there, or as if we pressed some buttons here and it would sound there.

When a yogi has discerned these differences and learned to know the principles beyond the objects he has also learned what is beyond sound, for in sound itself there is also some spiritual content. In no language have words been just chosen randomly, but they have been conducted from sounds in the principles themselves. Thus a yogi is able to understand sounds. Animals converse more simply than men but a yogi can tell from their voices what is going on in their minds.

Then Patanjali discusses a very remarkable attainment. A yogi can learn to make himself, his body invisible. It sounds very simple when Patanjali says: "By meditating on the shape of the body, by turning off senses and preventing the colours of the body to affect the eyes a yogi will become invisible." – This is scientifically said. Our body reflects light and another person sees this light. So nothing else is needed than preventing this light from reflecting. This is very hard to understand unless we hold on to the fact that according to yogic philosophy seeing and being seen is always about light. Both the eyes and the body have light. If there is no light then nothing is seen. If you can turn off this light then the other cannot see. So if you affect another's light by turning it off he cannot see. This happens by placing a dark light around another. A yogi can affect all senses of another person, he can prevent the functioning of all his senses. Some commentators state that this is a later addition, and we can understand their view because this sounds like hypnotism. We know that such an effect is possible with hypnotism. But a yogi does not do this; he will not manipulate or hypnotize anyone; he will completely leave another person undisturbed as a spiritual being. That is part of a yogi's ethics and moral. This sutra is original but it means such an attainment that the yogi manipulates light and not the senses.

I can list a few more attainments. When a yogi meditates on friendship, kindness, compassion and pity he will reach the attainment that he can spread happiness around him, and it will also affect in such a way that people will like him. One commentator claims that if he desires the friendship of any particular person he would gain it because he meditates upon all these beautiful virtues. He obtains love and can make another happy. – If then a yogi for example meditates on an elephant he will gain the strength of an elephant. By meditating upon any matter, near or far, small or great he can gain knowledge of them.

Then follow very detailed explanations. By meditating on the sun a yogi will gain knowledge of different planes, worlds. By meditating on the Moon he will gain knowledge of the solar system. This explains us why astronomy was such an advanced science in ancient India. They did not have all the instruments we have; all was accomplished with yoga. They knew very precisely all such things as the movements of Earth and the Sun.

When a yogi meditates on his navel chakra ie. nerve cluster – the *solar plexus* as it is also called – he will gain knowledge of the structure of the physical body. By meditating on the throat chakra the yogi will gain knowledge of the arisal of thirst and hunger, and will conquer them. By meditating on the transmitting channel in the etheric organism, the stream of prāna, the yogi will gain firmness and immobility of the body. He needs not do or prepare anything, he just focuses his thoughts on a certain point and his body will remain immobile. And when he meditates on the central nervous system in the head he will find out the light of the head and will then see gods wandering and moving. By meditating on this light the yogi will gain knowledge of anything he desires. This means knowledge beforehand. – If the yogi meditates upon his heart he will see the chitta and learn to know it.

IX
THE HIGHEST GOAL OF A YOGI

Patanjali devotes the fourth and final chapter of his book to the highest attainments of yoga, the highest in both form and content. And actually he seems to have had in his mind the final goal of yoga, for he has named this final chapter *kaivalya*, which means detachment and absoluteness.

The first sentence of Patanjali's in this last chapter is translated as: "The siddhis (this word is used to describe supernatural abilities in general; perfections, as they are translated in European languages) are attainable by different means: they can be attained either as natural gifts, by birth or by help of herbal potions and lotions, or by spells, mantras, or by asceticism." – In all these ways can supernatural abilities be attained. With this sentence Patanjali shows his wisdom and richness of knowledge: he knows that people try to attain supernatural abilities through different means. Abilities are in themselves such that they can arouse wants and desires in man. There may arise in man a desire to attain supernatural abilities, and he is ready to use whatever means necessary. He wants for example to become clairvoyant, to be able to fly in a different world, and he is ready to use whatever means necessary, whether they be good or bad.

Attainment of such abilities is no goal of yoga; in yoga they are attained naturally. Patanjali states that they can be obtained in many ways and he values them thus nearly worthless. We know that during the middle-ages in Europe witches used all kinds of herbal potions and lotions to enter another world. By using those their bodies stiffened and they flew off in their invisible bodies and did not know that their physical body was left behind. They went to a place where they had together all sorts of witches' sabbaths. Many used these kinds of ways out of plain curiosity to gain these abilities. The fact that these ways were not so great was shown in that these people tended to become eccentric and had to retreat to solitude for people started abhorring them. They were persecuted too severely and unnecessarily; most of them were such as are now called mediums. The people who at that time awakened those abilities in themselves were born the next time as mediums. If there are such people in our time we can assume that they have striven for such things earlier on. Of course it can be also so that one is innocent for one's abilities, in the meaning that he has not tried to obtain them by wrong means but they can be hereditary to him; they can be in his family's blood. And when this is so, it is vital that such a person will start to meditate in this life.

Patanjali mentions one more way, which is the awakening of abilities through spells, mumbling something to achieve a special bodily state. – There is also one way, although Patanjali does not mention it, i.e. the one used by so called primitive people and Muslims: dancing. The dervishes dance and spin around fast and thus obtain momentarily supernatural senses.

Then Patanjali mentions the way that has been common and known everywhere, i.e. asceticism, self-torture – hatha yoga. This will awaken those abilities in man. But all these ways Patanjali deems inferior for he adds: "With all these ways man will not obtain any permanent abilities." – They are all fleeting, they belong to his mortal personality, they do not reach the inner person which remains outside of them. Those abilities vanish when one dies. In our learned culture a respected and able person who has stuffed himself, his mind, full of all kind of knowledge, has read a lot of books, has tremendous memory – and modern civilization reveres him as a wonderful person – is in the end a very mortal being who takes nothing along with him to another life. All this knowledge vanishes in death; he is left only a certain amount of capacity to concentrate and advanced capability of remembering. Yet this knowledge is not to be looked down upon, on the contrary, but they are no eternal achievements one should strive for.

A yogi is a person who does not value so greatly things that are fleeting. Therefore he will obtain all kinds of abilities which enable him to know what he wants. A yogi can be as knowledgeable on factual matters as any of our professors. If a yogi does not know our vocabulary he might not know how to converse, but if he will get a hold on the professor's thought he will then be able to pass clear appraisals of things. Our scientific knowledge is really rather uncertain. Its views can change according to new discoveries, but this precisely is extremely good for it shows that we can progress. But this is slow progress and regards the material world. A yogi travels an inner path; he can observe things from within.

Patanjali says that all true knowledge and perfect life exist. A yogi's task is to establish a connection with this great stream of knowledge and of perfect life. Then can he act differently. If someone uses these other methods that were mentioned he is like the farmer who tries to irrigate his field by carrying to it water from the lake with his hands. But one who starts to practice yoga is like the farmer who digs ditches to his field so that the water from the lake can flow in them. He removes the obstacles from the way so the water will flow by itself. Thus a yogi does not need to strive for any specific supernatural attainments, for it would be like trying to grasp something from the stream of life with your hand. He does not need to think about any formal attainments; he just opens himself up as a channel for the great stream of knowledge and life. And Patanjali says: "Man cannot be rid of his imperfections, flaws and vices by thinking 'now I must get rid of this and this flaw; it must be rooted out'. This will accomplish nothing, man will not be free in such a way, but he must let all virtues flow into him; this will remove all imperfections from him."

We know it to be common that the spiritually less experienced people will say: "You must remove this flaw from yourself; God will not accept it." And one will become desperate when he cannot be rid of it; it only becomes worse when he tries to. Therefore he will say: "If there is no Redeemer, man will not accomplish anything." – And therefore there is a mechanical redeemer in the Christendom which atones everyone's sins with God. Most people think like this. – I have now spoken about the external part, not the internal.

Patanjali discusses also in this fourth part yoga's formally highest attainment, before he actually discusses its goal. He says: "The formally highest attainment is *mahāvideha*, and it is of two varieties. When it starts to develop on its own it first takes the *kalpita*-form and then the *akalpita*. Mahāvideha is the great stepping out, and creation of the magical body." This means, as spoken of in our time: the stepping out of his body and working outside of it. This acting is based on the fact that there is a vehicle in which to act. Therefore there are two sides to this stepping out of the body: stepping out and acting.

Now every man – realistically speaking – moves out of his body in his sleep; his consciousness descends to the back of his head and then to the spinal cord. If the nerves of the brain are in such a condition that they hold on to consciousness one cannot sleep. Sleeping is that consciousness is momentarily released from the shackles of the physical body. It can happen that the consciousness remains in the body so that the sleep is seeing all kinds of dreams, or it can get out so that man can rest and improve his bodily condition. During the day the body has been under a state of stress, so during sleep the body and a certain part of man will fix this disorder. For this to be possible to take place the personal waking consciousness has to be outside of the body.

But is the deep dreamless sleep always the same as functioning outside of the body? – Most people are in a state of lethargy in their consciousness as they sleep, not like being unconscious but in a way that their consciousness is exhausted and without thoughts, or so that it does not skim through memories. But a few people – and perhaps even great many among the civilized and other people – are somewhat conscious when outside of their bodies. The more they are conscious the more they can reach outside of their bodies; the connection with the body is not so firm. Everyone who becomes a theosophist will quite soon notice that their dream life is changing and that they start remembering peculiar things about their nightly life. He will be dealing with different people and visit places he has never seen in his waking consciousness. And he can make a peculiar observation that when he enters a strange town or place, it feels oddly familiar. This is all due to the fact that when one becomes a thinking being, one who thinks more than just the everyday matters, his dream life will become richer and freer. And when we examine the soul while the body sleeps, we notice that it moves in the astral world. It is of a bit vague shape, although it has taken with it the image of the physical body.

Even the savage peoples know that man flies in his sleep, for the more advanced people amongst them, like shamans etc. know this. Our learned men laugh at this but the common folk believe it. And they can tell that they have seen this and this dead person while sleeping. Some might say that it predicts rain, but most people do believe that they have met dead people.

When a yogi studies things he notices that dead people really exist and that man exists while sleeping. If we are scientifically accurate and narrow-minded we would have to say that man does not exist in his sleep; man who has not existed in dreams has not existed at all. Man dies and is born again. But the fact is that he exists while sleeping

105

as he exists when he has died, and will be born again on earth. Therefore we can understand so well what the yogi's achievement is. Instead of letting this time in his sleep being spent in unconsciousness and in vain, this time as well must made a "day" of action. It means that the yogi must create for himself a vehicle, a body, while being in this other state. – "The highest formal attainment of a yogi", says Patanjali, "is to create a body in which he is fully conscious and has total control of. It has two degrees: *kalpita* and *akalpita*. Kalpita is that the yogi with his meditation – the new body is not created while sleeping – creates kalpita mahāvideha." This means that the yogi in meditation creates himself this new body, just like a new chitta, he sort of detaches his chitta from himself, his thought and emotional aura.

Let us think of a yogi who sits in a meditation posture. He sends out his chitta but he is still in the physical body; he cannot get out of his body remaining self-aware so he sends out his chitta equipping it with partial consciousness. He will, for example say: "Now must this task be done, you must go there and complete that task." – His chitta will obey and act. And a yogi will take care of verifying for himself whether his chitta has acted out; as a seeker of truth he will find out whether the chitta has completed the ordered task.

Then when the yogi has obtained this kalpita mahāvideha he will begin to transform it to akalpita mahāvideha. This means that instead of remaining in his physical body he himself goes out in his chitta. His own personal consciousness leaves the physical body in a meditation posture and exists in this chitta, and uses the abilities the chitta has. And when the yogi has obtained this in his meditation he will have the same ability while sleeping, not otherwise. But Patanjali says that it is exactly the achieving of this ability that will banish all the shrouds that veil the light – it will demolish the veils from the light. And the shroud concealing the light is the emotional body of man, the body of suffering, pleasure and action. It is, as we call it in theosophical terms, the astral-mental body – and also the physical-etheric body.

A lot is said in this sentence of Patanjali's, for the innermost essence of man is light, and man's true life is in the light and the world of light. It is said in a holy book that God lives in the light. This depicts the truth a yogi will face, this wondrous truth that cannot be depicted by mundane words. In the light is the true home of man, and in these mahāvideha efforts the yogi will wipe out the veil shrouding the light. The bodies that the yogi naturally is left with will be transformed and become like obedient servants, instruments without any personal will. The yogi will then become a higher human being, an angel, a god who uses this human organism. That is why Patanjali states that in these efforts the yogi will attain a heavenly sense; he will shine; all his lower vehicles will also shine. He will gain an ability to move about in the world of light itself; he will gain control of the elements; he will gain firmness, strength, power over senses, also the ability to step into another body. – About this we will say a few words.

We know that every mediumistic person has had the experience that a foreign consciousness can take over him. People who are "sleeping preachers"* are just like such that a dead person can take over their bodies. A medium is a person whose connecting bond between the different vehicles is not firm. There are dead people in the after world who wish to give information to the living, and therefore they may use the body of a living person. In the other world there are dead who have been trained to be able to subtly take over a medium's body without causing any major disturbances. But this method is immoral, for when the dead visit the medium they hypnotize him and order him out of his body. Therefore a lone medium can either struggle to remain as himself or leave his body. It is also so that a medium willingly goes into a trance and sort of calls the dead to him.

*A Christian person who preaches, prophesies or addresses a public audience while "sleeping," that is, in a state of trance. (Editor)

107

A yogi achieves a true ability to use another person's body, if this person is out of his body whether in his sleep or in a trance. And we can thank this ability for the protection of mankind; for it would be a tremendous mess if there were no yogis who have taught how to safely utilize another person's body. There has also been a development amongst the dead. For as mankind evolves so do the circumstances in the after world. The dead are no longer idiots, they have not lost themselves. The more civilized the mankind, the more civilized the afterlife; people also seek knowledge there. Some can be attached to their own desires, but not everybody. There are many among the dead people who have been thinkers and researches on earth; they take this ability to the beyond. Although worldly matters are forgotten they retain this intellectual ability. One who has been an avid seeker of truth has a strong desire and love for truth also on the other side, and such a person is willing to take guidance. And there has been an awakening in the realm of the dead: "Is it not a pity that people in the world have such a wrong picture of the life after death? Could we not communicate something to them?" – What would have followed from that is that the dead would have wanted to try to reach us and communicate with us, and who knows what disturbances might have occurred unless some yogis, occultists, adepts had not noticed that in order to be able to help people this work must be organized. It is only beginning but will become a great influence in the next century; more and more people will come into contact with dead people.

Therefore it is good that nature gifts a yogi with such an ability. And a yogi who can create new bodies and work invisibly around the world does not accumulate any new karma. Patanjali says: "Work for the benefit of mankind will not create any new karma for the yogi." This is true help; it does not create new karma, and the scientific reason for it is that all these new chittas, new bodies are created from the self of the yogi. Patanjali says that the actions of all men are black, white, or in between; mostly in between. With a yogi none of that applies; he is aware of all the seeds and the results they lead in, so he does not create any karma.

But the final attainment, goal, to which a yogi's efforts in reality aim for is independence, liberty, absoluteness, omniscience. He must become absolutely god-like for whom nothing is hidden. And this develops gradually in such a way that his consciousness expands, it covers ever greater areas. He becomes aware of even more beings, living people, plants, dead people, gods – all these will enter him, will live in him. Patanjali is correct in saying: "There would be a tremendous confusion if the personal consciousness of all those living beings would be revealed to the yogi; then there would be no difference between the yogi's divine self and the selves of the others. Instead the yogi will only know their state, the level of evolution of their soul, but not what is going on in their minds."

This is great nobility of spirit. We see how a yogi is aware of what is civilization and finesse. Nature itself raises him to nobility. No curiosity belongs to a yogi. The more his consciousness is capable of holding within the more all sorts of curiosity is distanced from him. A yogi in his omniscience is not someone who would pry the secrets of others, who would know what goes on in someone else's mind. He knows the condition of other person's soul, on what point of evolution he is. In lower stages of evolution, when super sensory abilities awaken, they are such that they can arouse one's curiosity; they can penetrate another's aura. A truly wise one will be free of such things. How could he be interested in such things; how could they touch him in any way! Every person takes care of his own personal affairs in this life; a yogi's task is only to help every soul, and only therein comes to question the evolutionary level of the soul, from where the person has to advance onwards.

When a yogi has discerned the difference between purusha, i.e. spirit, and the finest of sattva-matter, then his knowledge will rise towards the great liberation. Purusha, spirit, is the only thing that is fulfilling for a yogi, not even the highest, finest of forms. In his final life the yogi is not interested even of the functions of intellect.

Patanjali's presentation ends with the words: "Because the yogi is no longer interested in any kind of forms his samādhi transforms into a cloud of dharma, of virtues, and from this cloud a shower of knowledge rains on thirsting souls – and he becomes one with God." – And now we can understand when another holy book says that: "When I return I shall come in a cloud of the sky." – The yogi is transformed into a cloud of virtues; in this he receives Christ.

X
THE REQUIREMENTS OF
SPIRITUAL KNOWLEDGE

In all times, – we can practically say, – most people have believed that man exists after death, and that there is an invisible spirit world alongside of this visible world. The majority of people still believe this today. But most people have the opinion that these things are and will be mere speculation and nothing can be known of them.

There have been various different beliefs about man's life after death. Everywhere there have been some kind tales about it; people have not only said that man exists after death but his state of being has also been described; and in some places in certain times it has been believed that man remains in this spirit world when he has died. This is what Christendom usually believes. Sometimes it is believed that man remains in the spirit world only for a brief period of time only to return back on Earth. But like said, although these things have been described very vividly most people believe that nothing can be known about them; they are and will remain matters of faith. Therefore it is usually understood that it is precisely religion that deals with these subjects of the spirit world, which is in itself a matter of faith. But when we have studied old civilizations and old religions, and examined their original writings and the lives and words of their founders we have become convinced that all the greatest men who have appeared on the face

111

of the earth, and who have founded religions and deeply delved into their secrets, they all have assured as some assure today that there is certain knowledge attainable by man. This knowledge is the knowledge of God, of truth, as it is also said. This knowledge transforms man, for when he learns to know God and learns to know the truth then the eternal life enters him, as it is said – or he enters into eternal life. Then the eternal life has opened up to him; the eternal life has been born in him. This is a wonderfully magnificent, exalted and peculiar process, so claim all the greatest exponents of mankind. And we could say that even those people who do not have such experiences but do think for themselves, like philosophers, they too feel that they could understand such knowledge and its validity, but in general they do not presume that such knowledge could be possible. "Of course it is only imagination what those unusual people have experienced; it could not have been real knowledge. They call it knowledge but of course they have imagined it, and now imagine accordingly to have learned to know God. But that is nonetheless very peculiar and interesting; it would be excellent if man could gain such knowledge." Philosophers could understand this theoretically.

Philosophers usually divide the world, into two; they talk about matter and spirit. They talk about the material, visible, manifested world and then about spirit, the world of spirit, consciousness. They say that there are two things in the world that cannot be denied: matter that has dimension, and consciousness, which is an altogether different reality; consciousness that functions in matter and through matter, but is such a different reality that philosophers regard it as a mystery. The philosophers do not understand how these two subjects relate and interact with each other. We know that this is exactly the question the philosophers have troubled themselves with, how consciousness can affect matter and manifest via matter. We know that some philosophers have become materialists and said that consciousness is born out of the movements of matter; materialists believe that there is only one reality, matter and that consciousness is born of it. It is like a liquid that has been excreted from matter. Consciousness has been excreted from the brain like some other liquid is excreted in the human body. This is the conclusion that materialists have arrived to and think that the riddle is solved. But instead those who have thought a bit more rigorously, who have considered more details have to smile gently at the materialists. These people say that consciousness is a reality in its own right and that it could not have been born of matter. They are totally different realities, for matter has dimensions; it is dependent of time and space, but consciousness is not dependent of time and space. Consciousness can travel anywhere in space, independent of location; it can go back in its memory, it can reveal the past and gaze into the future, look behind the curtain, see what will happen. Consciousness is a strange reality, totally different than the material reality. So say these philosophers who think and know that it is not possible that consciousness could be born out of matter. But because consciousness is altogether so different from matter how can their relationship to each other be understood? What an achievement would be, these philosophers say, if man could attain real knowledge of consciousness, if he could solve the mystery of consciousness, if he could break the shackles of matter and become limitless living consciousness, if he could solve the mystery of the absolute? There can be only one reality manifesting in two ways, as some philosophers say, like the old philosophers of India. It is like entering a temple when we approach and old Indian philosopher, and when he says that one is absolute, one absolute life. It manifests as spirit and matter, consciousness and manifested form, but only one reality is behind it. If one could know this reality he would then have solved the mystery of the essence of consciousness and the essence of matter. And when some people have said that they have learned to know God, have attained knowledge of God, truth, they have meant exactly that they have solved the mystery of consciousness. What is God? Consciousness. Consciousness is God manifest. Consciousness is thought, consciousness is reason, consciousness is will, consciousness is the life that is in matter and affects in matter. If we can really attain knowledge of God, get to know God then we must solve the mystery of existence. Philosophers acknowledge this but naturally doubt whether such a result can be reached. And then of course all people and philosophers laugh at dubious knowledge. They cannot comprehend any other kind of knowledge that this philosophical, synthetic knowledge of consciousness and God, or knowledge of the visible world. They cannot understand any other world. They do not actually understand much else about existence. If man exists after death, then of course his consciousness remains. If it can exist as a consciousness without a physical body then he can exist also after death, which is a very problematic issue. They cannot understand anything like that for they think that consciousness is bound to matter; consciousness manifests through matter; and when matter ceases to exist so does consciousness. And therefore it is best to be doubtful about life after death. Individuality cannot exist when the matter through which the personality has lived and manifested disappears. And yet always it has been believed that man does exist after death. The belief of all times is that the spirit world exists. And the philosophers laugh at the spirit world: "And we should believe in ghosts in the spirit world. They're all bedtime-stories. Man has a natural urge to remain in existence. I do not want to die in death, I want to exist. That is the natural selfishness of man and therefore he imagines that he would exist after death." So say the scientist-philosophers. – Also in our Christianity it has always been thought that one cannot know anything about this, one must only believe. A Christian can talk about that God can be known, but one cannot know anything about life after death, one must simply believe what is said in the holy book. So has been claimed by Christianity for centuries. Therefore people have grown into this conviction that there is no knowledge, only belief. But recently and especially after Madame Blavatsky founded the Theosophical movement the idea has spread that knowledge regarding life after death and the spiritual world can also be obtained. That is a very extraordinary claim. And most civilized people naturally abandon this thought. How could it be possible? – But nature itself has risen to proclaim: "Behold! There is knowledge of heaven, of the spiritual world, about things you cannot straight away explain." – Spiritistic movement has since the last century convinced through mediums, especially sensitive people the spiritual world can be known. And it has been verified that all other explanations excluding the presence of the spirit world, the presence of a dead person, all such have no foundation. It is hard to explain things otherwise than that dead people are participating, that man does exist after death. This is not a commonly acknowledged thing, but people in the scientific circles are starting to feel that there are more and more mysterious things that cannot be explained. There are such phenomena as telepathy, the transference of thought from one person to another. That is a proven phenomenon. How is it understandable then if only the visible matter is believed in, that a man even when far away can transmit a thought to another? It is a well-proven fact that if someone is a competent hypnotist and another person a medium, then even if the Hypnotist was in London and the medium in Paris, and if the hypnotist would say "sleep" the medium would sleep. This shows that there exists influence at distance between men. The mere existence of radio with its peculiar invisible waves – when we are beginning to see everything surrounded by invisible forces – has the effect that the scientific world cannot ignore these things. Even though one would not have studied the principles behind radio he still could have heard a concert from Helsinki even if he himself lived in the countryside, or he could have heard a concert from London, and he must confess that there exists a wondrous influence at a distance through the air.

If we now observe impartially and objectively the problem of knowledge in general we can state in advance that there surely exists one true knowledge, but at the same time there exists three kinds of varieties of knowledge. The first type of knowledge is obtained through the sensory world about the invisible world. This we all know. Then there is another type, absolute knowledge of truth and God, of life itself and its secret. Then there is a third kind of knowledge and this possibility is hard to deny, the knowledge of the things that are between this visible world and the absolute truth i.e. God. Clearly it is not so that there would only be this visible world and God behind it, as the protestant world has believed, that man dies and is buried and then is awoken to life with God in heaven. The Protestants do not believe in ghosts and such. In the catholic world people believe in saints and they are prayed to, and they think that there is a hell and a purgatory and God in the distance, but nothing in between. But the Protestants place God immediately after the visible world so that there is no space in between. But lately it people have started to think that it seems like there is something more than this visible world. There is an invisible world, a world of mysteries, and one might obtain knowledge about that too. So it is possible to obtain three kinds of knowledge: knowledge of the invisible world, knowledge of God i.e. truth, and knowledge of the invisible world between God and the visible world. And if there so exists three sorts of knowledge we can ask how can we obtain knowledge of all these worlds? Then naturally our attention draws to the spiritual world, the state between God and the visible world. There are states in the spiritual world which we call purgatory and heaven, which are way stations on our journey to God. We wonder how we can obtain knowledge of all of them for it has always been believed that one cannot obtain any knowledge of them. But it is as if life itself proclaimed that knowledge can be obtained of all of these matters. So we ask: how do we obtain this knowledge? A thought occurs to us spontaneously that if the spirit world can be approached then it can be done in two ways. From this visible world we can sort of ascend to the spiritual world, sort of step into the spiritual world; as if see upwards and into the invisible world from this visible world. Or the other way is to descend into the invisible world, but this requires first knowledge of God, knowledge of life itself and its manifestation. These two ways undoubtedly exist. This we understand for certain if we can experience in our mind these different worlds and varieties of knowledge. To a man it of course feels most natural that he would reach the spirit world and the knowledge of it by ascending and entering into it from this visible world. Perhaps only a few might feel that one needs knowledge of God first and then perhaps one could get knowledge of other things. For it is as if one would need an exceptional mentality to first look for the knowledge of God. It feels so natural to think: "Here I am now in the visible world but would need knowledge whether man exists after death. For if man exists after death it is something natural. Even if the spiritual world exists how do we know God exists." – If one is a great philosophical mind he will not adopt such an attitude. He will naturally want to know whether a spiritual world exists, and if he then sees that it exists, and if he sees that also he himself exists after death this may give him faith in God, and so he becomes convinced that God exists because there is an invisible world; there is an order in the world, some rational, holy order. But if man does not exist after death, if there is no spirit-world, if we just die off after being here for awhile then what good will it do to talk of God. One thinks very naturally in such a way, and he might have a scientific thirst for knowledge that drives him to seek knowledge of the invisible world. – Now let it be stated here that all the wise ones, the wisest of all, have said the same what Jesus has said: "But seek you first the kingdom of God, and his righteousness; and all these things shall be added to you." All the wise people have said that if you seek first God, this great, fundamental truth, life itself, then you shall obtain knowledge of other things as well, but if you seek other things first, no matter how mysterious, you will not receive help from life, and the world is filled with dangers. Of course we don't heed much this kind of counsel, but let us take note that the wisest of people have said so.

117

If we reflect this for ourself we can understand there is an invisible world and then also understand what this invisible world is like, and also understand why is it dangerous.

If you think the problem of knowledge or about human capability for knowing in this visible world you come to the conclusion that it is based on sensations. Through our senses we gain knowledge of the visible world. But that is no real knowledge; all scientists and philosophers will admit it. Having sensations and making observations of the surrounding world is not knowledge, but knowledge comes from knowing how to organize these observations. The prerequisite for knowledge is thinking and reasoning. Also animals make observations, an animal can see, hear and feel but we have no certain proof that an animal would know. We can clearly see that man has knowledge. Man's experiences are different, or actually they are the same as an animal's but he can form knowledge from these experiences for he is a rational being, for he thinks, for in him is the thinker, intellect which enables him to know. We have sensations and observations we categorise and conceptualise them, make notions, reflect and reach an understanding of the natural laws which govern this world. If we did not have intellect, memory and knowledge we could be horrified when the sun sets; but our experience and knowledge tells us that in due time the sun will rise again. – But senses of man are deceitful. Man has with scientific calculations and observations come to the certainty that the sun does not rise or set even though it would seem so. Our sense perceptions like that have been proved false. Our knowing can surpass sense perceptions. We have reached a point in our knowledge that when we think about this visible world, and reflect what we know about it we in fact come to the conclusion that this visible world is a sensory illusion. Ask any scientist whether this chair represents reality and he will answer that it is an illusion. We can hear it when we knock on it and feel and see it. We all feel and see in the same way but we must admit to ourselves that it is a complete illusion, for this reality as it appears to our consciousness does not exist as such. It is only our notion of reality but it is not reality itself, das Ding an sich*. A natural scientist talks about atoms. He tells us right away that this chair is assembled of multitudes of atoms. Atoms are mysterious things. What is the secret behind everything, what is reality? It is that there are tiny entities, remarkably tiny and invisible entities that cannot be seen even with the greatest of microscopes, but they exist; so has been calculated. The atoms are at a distance from each other. This chair is a big composite of little solar systems; there are countless of them. Time and space are illusion, size is an illusion. How could we know anything if everything is our illusion and nescience? If we had a different way of perceiving, the solar system could be as small as possible; space does not really exist in any other way than as a mode in our consciousness. It can be small or so vast that we have not the faintest of idea, but relatively this solar system in the chair is smaller than the solar system we live in; in abstract thought there is no size. We have nothing else but knowledge of illusions. This chair is assembled of countless numbers of solar systems and they are kept together by a mysterious force. It is life and movement. Natural scientists admit that life is movement. All our notions from this visible world actually depend on movement. Movement is life. If there were no life – movement – it would not be possible to sense anything. Then everything would be as if dead. But existence is life, is movement, is vibration, it is the circling of those solar systems, the movement of those solar systems, those atoms. This is what makes perception possible. – We can take scientific proofs regarding everyday life showing that movement makes illusions possible. For example if we hear pistol shots, 15 shots a second, then we hear 15 shots. But if we hear 16 separate shots in one second we no longer hear them as separate shots but we hear them as one sound: our ear perceives only one

---

*Immanuel Kant: Critique of Pure Reason ("das Ding an sich") Thing-in-itself. (Editor)

continuous sound. Let us take a scientific example regarding our sight. If we have a gas flame which can be ignited and extinguished six times per second, we can see it igniting and extinguishing. But if it is ignited and extinguished seven times a second we only see one flame. Because then it becomes a coherent phenomenon; the movement is so fast that we cannot see the movement but the phenomenon which we have created. – Let us take another example. We have a faucet at the altitude of 500 meters. The faucet is opened so that a stream size of a finger streams down. The water travels so fast that if we took an axe and tried to cut the stream, we could not make it budge. The running of water is so fast and so coherent and hard; even harder than a tree; the movement makes it so. Everyone also knows that if we have a bicycle and it has spokes, we can see every spoke if the speed is slow, but when the speed accelerates, we no longer see any spokes. But even thought the spokes were very thin and the wheel very narrow, we could not throw anything through it for all would ricochet back. Such illusions we have in everyday life. The whole visible world is composed of such illusions. We also know that sound is vibration. But behind the sounds we perceive there is something nonexistent which to us is silence. In nature there are vibrations that are either above or below the voices we can hear. Sometimes sound changes into light; we see greatly differing colours, red has the widest, violet the shortest wavelength. What are the colours indigo and ultraviolet? We know that in colour photography we try to capture ultraviolet colour and thus see something that vibrates faster than the other colours we can perceive. The whole world is vibration but we only perceive a part of it, some fragments from the whole vibratory scale. It is light and sound, and a part of it is heat for example. Our knowledge of the visible world is remarkably limited. Naturally we understand that if a ghost, a dead person, a spirit exists, all it needs is to have its body vibrate similarly to our bodies, and in such a way that our senses can perceive these vibrations, and then this spirit being can exist to us.

But if the colours of this ghost are ultraviolet, higher in the vibratory scale than the colour violet, then this creature is invisible. Our hand goes through his body unhindered. This is not a supernatural thing but a natural conclusion.

There is yet another perspective we know of the visible world. Do we seek knowledge of the world? Not really. The world rushes on our senses without us having to do anything. One must shut his eyes and ears for not to perceive this world, for the visible world enters man and tells him "Do you not wish to know me, to find out what I am?" – As men we cannot move about in darkness and claim we cannot know anything about life for the whole world enters us. This is a very important thing for it explains us what is meant by the saying that the invisible world can become dangerous to us. Let us presume that there would be a way – and people have always found out that there is such a way – with which we could make our senses so subtle that our eyes would open to the invisible world. And we would have a sense that would function through these physical eyes and that our eyes would be so refined that they could see ultraviolet rays, perhaps sense colours beyond the spectrum of red and sense that reality. Let us presume that our eyes would evolve like that. (But let us presume that our eyes would not learn to receive all the new colours when they open up to a new world.)We see the invisible world, into the ultraviolet world, which at first is a bit foggy, a little silvery, shining in totally new combinations of colours. In this world move about the deceased and spirits and probably a whole host of other creatures. Why would they, the spirits, the deceased be alone in this world? No, there are other beings; there are different creatures, not just humans. Now that our eyes open to the invisible world we notice that it enters into us straight away, it rushes on us. In this visible world there are a lot of conflicts and dangers. Some wild beast could attack me and anything could happen. As they say, the unexpected always happens. The invisible world is similar. As there are wild beasts here, so are there such also. When my eyes open up to the invisible world, and I know nothing yet then,

121

and all kinds of monsters assault me and laugh that there is a creature who knows nothing. This is all natural, there is nothing inexplicable there. Many people while reading from the books of the wise the admonition that "you should not develop supernatural abilities", – may have thought that what harm could possibly befall me. He does not understand that he could be in danger. How could there be dangers, more than anywhere else, like here on Earth. He knows how to protect himself for sure, he thinks. But it is very difficult to protect one's self even here on Earth if one is assaulted by some wild beast in a South-American jungle. One can have learned to take care of himself in the visible world but it does not mean he could manage in the invisible world. Therefore it is a lot safer not to end up in that world unprepared. Therefore the wise ones have said: "If you take this path ascending from below, stepping from the visible world into the invisible one, then remember that you must have a teacher and a guide who knows and who can teach you." This was the path in the old mysteries, and then a hierophant worked as a guide. It is said in the Upanishads of old India that: "Find yourself a teacher, for without him it is very dangerous for you to undertake this path."

This path has always existed, but after Jesus Christ there is another path that is closer to all of us; a path which to a modern man might feel a bit strange and uncomfortable: "Seek you first the kingdom of God." This path has also existed always, but after Jesus Christ it has really existed for everybody. People who do not wish to or cannot take this path can then settle in scientific research, for the safety of scientific research is that it proceeds slowly and taking every detail into account. Scientific research is now moving from visible world into the invisible world. The investigation regarding the spiritistic movement is taking the scientific research step by step into the invisible world. In this there are also dangers but then the dangers are learnt to be seen and conquered, for in science everything happens so slowly.

But if one wishes to proceed faster, if he is not satisfied

with mankind knowing after perhaps 10 million years something about the invisible world, if he now wants to attain knowledge of truth then this other path will open up for him: Learn to know that the great life, divine life, the great consciousness, which we call God is in you too. God is in you as well, the redeemer is in you. You are a son of God. Learn to think about this. Learn to penetrate, focus on this, own the thought that you are the child of the universe, announcement of infinity, a Son of God. Learn to identify with this, and when you try to identify with this you will no doubt understand, and this will happen as of its own accord, that that which is ugly, selfish, animal, must fall away. How can you, a Son of God who is identifying with this fact, how could there be anything weak, evil or sinful in you? This all must fall off. You understand this even beforehand. But then happens an amazing rebirth, of which the wise ones speak of, in which you find out and see, feel and know that you truly are a Son of God and that Father in heaven is behind existence and that the Father is love, and that therefore love is behind the whole existence. Love is the great bosom in which the whole existence rests. Start from this end, learn to know the Father, learn to know God, like Jesus said: "Seek you first the kingdom of God." When you first gain contact with the great Father of the world, when God becomes the redeemer in you, when Jesus has shown you this way and become the life and the truth for you, it is then – and is it any wonder – that the invisible world will step before you. And then you will have nothing to worry about for you are a Son of God, who is stepping into the invisible world to save it, as the visible world is also to be saved. The fact that you are a Son of God makes you understand this visible world. What do we understand of it when we only study the natural laws? It only becomes more mysterious and wonderful. And when our eyes open up to the invisible world and we see so many new details that we cannot organize all of them, then the problem of being becomes even more complicated and confusing. But when we are born again as sons of God, this visible life is instantly transformed into something else. We have understood it, its mystery is solved. We know what existence is, that life, the world is for us to save it; that people are for us to love. And why do we ourself exist? I exist because God exists, and God exists because He loves. Everything changes. The mystery of the visible life is solved and before our senses steps the invisible world, and we begin to study it even more. It will itself step before us and we will learn to know it always more. When we know God where are the hells and devils that could frighten us.

XI
BEYOND DEATH

I would like to talk about life after death. Not only because the matter is in itself important and fascinating to all of us, but also because we can find from it, like from all other philosophical and occult subjects of life, something new. We can make continuously new observations about life after death as well as other occult subjects, and then those subjects feel all new and wondrous so that again we wish to return to them. There are theosophists who think that there is nothing new under the Sun in this respect, so that when they have read a theosophical book, when they once have read about reincarnation and life after death, hell, purgatory and heaven they feel as if they knew already everything. They are not bothered or wish to read any other books because they think that those subjects are so familiar. If we speak so in our ignorance it shows firstly that we know nothing, and secondly that we are not yet real seekers of truth. For if we are seekers of truth who really wish to attain knowledge, we cannot think regarding any such great question like life after death that we would already know everything. On the contrary, we know clearly that we know nothing but we wish to gain knowledge. And the first step on the path of knowledge is to find out what others might possibly know. If one manages to figure this out then one has gained something, but will not stop there but still wants to hear about the same things, for there might always be some new word, or story, which might better clear up things and bring new perspectives. As a seeker of truth one always wishes that he could contact with another's soul, could hear what this other person might have experienced, would somehow gain access to his knowledge.

When one is a seeker of truth in this way he always discovers something new and will not tire of anything. We are very shallow if we get tired; we have only reached the surface and have not taken even the first step to really delve into anything. Life after death is such an issue that one can discuss it over and over again. After it has been discussed one may have had an experience or seen something which sheds light about it in a new into his soul, its destiny and evolution. Therefore it is natural that one wishes to delve over and over again into the question of life after death.

This time I would like to discuss a few things related this subject of life after death. First I would like to talk about the peculiar thing we could call the locality of the life after death. And second, the relation of the life after death to our visible, everyday life; I will talk about how they relate to each other and how we can perceive, understand what miraculous law governs the existence, how everything here is arranged in an exceptional way.

First about the locality of the post mortem life. We know that life after death does not take place in this visible world for we move out of it. Therefore there may be people who think that there is no life after death, because when a man dies the body is left behind here and the soul is nowhere to be seen. Therefore it is clear that the life after death must have a different locality. We know from our theosophical studies that this life after death is said to be both material and local. One becomes convinced of that in séances if one faces spiritual messaging and apparitions, but above all if one personally experiences life after death while still living here, if one is able to move outside of one's body in that other world in which the life after death is spent. Then it becomes clear that the life after death has its own locality and materiality, although they are not of physical quality and not in these three dimensions. This life after death can briefly be described metaphorically as such that at first it is lived in the Moon and then in the Sun. This is of course symbolically speaking for the life after death is naturally spent "inside" our own planet Earth, in the invisible organization. Just like we have this physical-etheric body and then our invisible aura, into which we end up in after our death and which forms the image of our physical personality, so does Earth have not only this physical-etheric body on the surface of which we live on – or we do not actually live on the surface for air is also physical, but on the coarse surface – so does Earth also have its astral body, its aura, its sphere and then also a kind of form of its self. I would rather not call it a mental body for I like to combine the mental and the astral body.,This organization of I is sort of outside the mental body; we could say that Earth has an organization of I which is a substantial entity shaped like a sphere.

When we examine both this I-sheath and astral body, we arrive at the odd sounding conclusion that Earth's astral aura reaches all the way to the Moon. It is as if the Moon, that orb which we see with our bare eyes in the sky would be within the sphere of Earth's astral aura and would circulate it and always remain within this sphere. And because the Moon has handed over its own life to Earth, – for it is older than our Earth, – it has no more an astral body or an organization of I. But it has some sort of astral vestige left, a seed which is in contact with Earth's astral body; it is much smaller so its radius intersects the other. The astral bodies of the Moon and Earth are in a sense connected. And the Moon has a tremendous effect on Earth; the Moon is like Earth's mother. It not only affects in a physical-etheric way, drawing the masses of water, but it also affects as a secret force in the astral aura of Earth including all beings that have an astral body – men and animals. In theosophical and old mystical books it is said that man's life after death is *sublunar*, subject to the Moon, belonging to the Moon. This

127

saying is not only symbolical but it is literally true, for as Earth's astral body is subject to the influence of the Moon, and when man after death enters the afterworld – *purgatory*, as the Catholics say, or *kāmaloka*, as the Orientals say, a place of purification – then man as a soul is under the influence of the Moon, the realm of the Moon. This is a very peculiar thing. It is also because of this that the old Indian literature speaks about Earth's lunar body, meaning its astral body. They also talk about the path which leads to the ancestors after death, i.e. to the Moon. These are mysterious remarks which are understood when one finds out about these things; that is that the astral life after death, which is spent in the astral body of the Earth is subject to the influence of the Moon. The latter part of the astral life, which is usually called lower heaven, is subject to the Moon and in the realm of the Moon. Then the human soul has reached that part in the astral body of Earth in which the astral body of the Moon is conjoined. – This will be cleared when we talk about the life after death of the human soul.

But then there is yet in the afterlife of man his actual heaven, and this heaven is in the organism of I of Earth, which we can also call Earth's solar body. This Earth's organism of I is remarkable in the way that it is as big as the whole solar system; to put it another way it is the Sun itself. In this physical life the Sun is up there in the sky and it looks like a distant glowing orb that illuminates us. When we enter this heaven, into the I-body of Earth, the solar body, it is as if we entered the Sun, but then we realize that the Sun is not just a tiny orb in the middle of the solar system, but it expands the whole solar system. In the I-body of Earth, which is the Sun itself, we cannot see any visible Sun, – which is merely the physical phenomenon, but we are within a light so powerful that it penetrates Earth. In this heavenly state, in the Sun itself, the light is everywhere, but still as if flooding inwards.

What comes to the lunar body, the lunar state which we enter when passing into the after world, there is, of course, no Sun but also no Moon in a way that it would shine in the sky, but we live within the sphere of the Moon so that everything shines. Therefore in the Middle-Ages was coined the word "astral" from the Latin word *aster*, which means a star. It is a starry world; everything there glows like the stars and the Moon in the night, in a pale but clear light; but the light is totally different from the light of the Sun. In the after world, in the lunar plane of Earth the lighting is very clear and bright, but it has a silvery tone and it appears to come out of nowhere, but everything shines of their own accord as if with a borrowed light. That is moonlight.

This is a tremendously interesting observation when it is done objectively. I have spoken about these things, as one might say, objectively, but a man who enters these worlds when he has died will be unable to make this kind of observations for he has not developed his own lunar or astral body so that he would know how to objectively make observations. When observations like these are now presented they are not portrayed from the viewpoint of a deceased, but of one who makes objective observations. We can say that the after death life starts when the sound of knockings is heard and doors are opened and closed. Man is no longer in the physical world but instead the doors have been opened to a new world, a lunar world, into which man enters; and when his state of being there is exhausted and he is allowed to enter a new plane knockings are heard again and doors are opened and closed. He enters a third great hall that is nothing but dazzling light, so dazzling that he could not bear it unless he were so pure, so purified that what is best in him has united with the higher self with which alone he is able to bear that light. Most people cannot yet bear this light for long, although in that state there is no time at all in our common in the sense we understand it, and we can say that a thousand years is but a day in that state.

In that heavenly body of Earth, in its organism of I, locality is such that because it comprises the whole solar system it at the same time encompasses all the planets within the solar system. This is a peculiar and notable fact. – And the situation is naturally the same with the other planets as well; the organism of I of every planet encompasses the Sun and all planets. It is a very amazing state of being, but even that is limited, form-bound, for it does not reach outside the solar system.

When we turn our attention to the other question I mentioned earlier: "What is the relation between man's visible and post mortem lives?", we see that in this visible life we spend a part of our time, usually it is said 2/3 of our life in the waking consciousness, but at night when we sleep our consciousness is not in this visible life but it is somewhere else. Scientific researchers have not found out where it is; it could be said that it is in the cerebellum or spine, but it does not explain what sleep is and what we are when we sleep. A third of our time we spend in a dream life, when we are retracted from the waking consciousness and after waking know nothing else of that dream life than the fact that we have dreamed. And a dream can be very confusing, crazy. But by saying so we prove that our waking consciousness was involved in the dream life. We wonder what is this world in which anything can happen, things we would not do in waking consciousness; and also such things can happen that do not exist in waking life. Thus we often regard dream life with disdain. Scientists began paying attention to the dream life only as later as during the 19th century, and it has been noticed that in it man reveals the state of his lower soul, psychoanalysts have become particularly discerning in this matter, so that if one reveals one's dreams to them, they are able to explain them so that one would be downright amazed. For example a doctor can on the basis of a dream help a patient so that he is freed from a psychological trouble, a complex. A practiced psychoanalyst can on the basis of dreams extract such things from the depths of another's soul that one could not have even expected them to exist, and so has been able to help him.

What we remember of our dream life is an insignificantly small portion of our entire nightly life, for it has been noticed that even a long dream has sometimes not lasted even a second, so the dream life must have had lots of such things that have remained hidden from us, of which we have no knowledge or recollection when we wake up. Only occultists who can observe these things in super-physical ways know a man's state when he is sleeping. They know that while a man sleeps he actually goes through the day's events; he watches them as dream images. The persons and events he has been dealing with during the day influence him and communicate with him as vividly as during the day, and he sees how he could have acted in different situations. He criticizes himself: "Here I did wrong". But this sort of judgment is more instinctual than self-conscious. In his sleep man enters a state in which things and events speak in their own way; he sees everything without being able to self-consciously think anything. He merely receives impressions; and it is as if his own Self within would react to them. And if this Self then feels there has been something good; if the Self has been able to take something for itself – this Self that can hold no evil – it then sends it back to this sleeping person, the astral body. From this follows that if one has had enough sleep, if he has slept long enough so that his sleep has been more than just going through past day's events, long enough for the Self to add something to it, he then feels refreshed; issues have been solved. Therefore the saying "Better to sleep on it" is very wise, for in his sleep man is dealing with the inner world and so matters will become clear to him, so that the next day he knows how things are to be resolved. We must not despise such proverbs which are based on experience. It is wise to sleep before making important decisions.

I will not discuss now what happens to man's physical body when he sleeps; this side we will now leave unattended. – The forces and laws which govern a man while he sleeps are of moral and not of physical quality like here. Here everything is highly organized. If we mix water with sugar it becomes sweet water, there is nothing particularly moral about that, as regards surface appearances. It is a different matter if we delve into it deep enough, but scientists see no

131

moral therein, only causal relationships following natural laws. But when man enters the Earth's astral body at night, the laws there are moral, not physical. Therefore when a man remembers something of the astral life, or something about the effect of his higher Self, or what is left in his brain of his past day, it all feels natural in the dream state. Whatever wonderful things would happen in his sleep, they all are bound by moral, not physical laws; they are astral, not physical.

When a man dies he is first put within the sphere of influence of the Moon and then the Sun. But we could say it otherwise. He is first dealing with night and then day. We can call the astral life night, "die Nachtseite der Natur"*, as one German philosopher has said. Truly this astral life and the astral body of earth, the whole life governed by the Moon is like a night-life, whereas the life governed by the Sun is like a day-life. Therefore we can say metaphorically: in post mortem life there is first a night-life and then a day-life.

When we observe a dying man we see that his "death" is that his etheric body, the inner part of the physical body, which normally is connected to the physical body, is detached and moves through the body from the feet to the head and departs the physical body – and man in his consciousness follows along. When this process starts man enters first a state in which his consciousness rises to the etheric brain – it does not remain in the physical brain. The person is as if in a trance, in a wonderful dream; you could think that he is sleeping but he is not – he could have his eyes open – he is in the special state of which those who know say that a dying man is not to be disturbed – do not cry next to him, do not move him. When he is in this state his whole life passes before his eyes objectively, like a film; and the person himself is totally objective; he is his own judge, he watches his own actions, words and thoughts.

---

*Gotthilf Heinrich von Schubert (1780-1860) (Editor)

Not disapproving nor approving, but in his feelings, but in his consciousness, in his thoughts objectively sorting out: these on the left being bad, these on the right being good. Then he discards his etheric body i.e. the etheric force. Therefore, even though he dies, it is often so that he continues that watching and judging in his etheric body, and it is as if he threw out into the world his old life, all those images he had formed during his earthly life, for from one point of view it is as if he saw images. It is as if he threw all those images out into the world to be devoured by the forces of the world, and by this he is liberated from the contents of his old personality. What happens then? – Three days have passed since he has discarded the etheric body. During that time he might have had some adventures. The deceased person is vividly animate in his etheric body and he participates in the world but we will not pay attention to that now. The rule is that a man discards his etheric body, his recollections to be devoured by the forces of the world, and these recollections deal with the waking life, for the etheric body has gathered day-time images during the earthly life.

Then one enters the Earth's astral body, the lunar body, enters the life after death, the after world. And the basis for this after-life is that one lives through his nightly life on Earth, that life which he has experienced in the lunar body while sleeping at night. And likewise as he remembered the day's events backwards from the moment he fell asleep until the morning when he woke up, so will he after death in the Moon-life begin from the moment of death and proceed backwards. We know that if we try to recall our life all the way to the moment when we entered this visible world from our mother's womb, we cannot remember the first few years in our waking consciousness. Our memory begins from the age of one or two, depending on how conscious of the world we were when we were young. But our night-time memory, what we have lived in our sleep – and as small children we sleep most of the time – our whole nightly life confronts us when we die. In the lunar body in the after-world we relive backwards our nightly life. Our nightly life was always a repetition of our daily life. Now in the after-world it is so in a new way; not objective observation but that purification which takes place through the dream images during sleep. This takes place again now after death in the after world. During dreaming we learn relatively little for it is not real for us, it is merely passive watching of mental images; but after death it is not only passive images, but what before were passive and in a sense unreal images now become real. There we are in a constant state of purification, we live daily life all the time, but not only that but also how the daily life influenced us during the night. All the people and events come to us vividly and speak to us, and we gain new kind of experiences when something we did had been wrong. This is no longer mere peaceful repeating of events but criticizing and analyzing one's character evaluating and selecting oneself; it is throwing one's self in the pains in as much there has been sin and evil in us. All this remembering is so real that it cannot be resolved in any other way than through unspeakable suffering and agony. We return all the way to our earliest childhood – and our journey backwards is a journey to ever greater purity – and then to the gates of birth and through them into that world and life which we lived before being born on Earth. Life in the after world also contains the recollection of the life which we lived before our birth, and this makes the after death life very interesting. There is a rather peculiar phase when in the after death life we come again into contact with those beings with whom we were in contact before being born. What kind of spiritual entities were they? They were those great teachers that we had known in the previous life, by whom we had been influenced, those old wise ones whose teachings we had heard in our previous life and who had blessed us when we had to descend once again from heaven back to Earth. But now we have naturally developed new personalities, so that when at the end of the afterlife we meet these teachers, it does not mean that we would remember our past earthly life; not at all, but we come to contact with them only because according the law of life they watched over our birth into this world.

Therefore the afterlife is very peculiar, for it is as if man travelled up from the Earth's surface out into space to the Moon. And in "the Moon" he will meet the great teachers whom he had trusted in his previous life. And this last phase is already a kind of heavenly state and it is called the lower heaven. There are the old teachers who had as it were given the basis for the state of our soul when we were born. In the way we tried to cultivate ourselves in the previous life – if this education and cultivation was consistent with a certain teacher – in that way we had moulded our soul before we were born here. Let us say that this is the first time we were born into Christendom and have heard of Jesus Christ; in the previous life we could have been in China and there we heard about Buddha and Confucius, visited temples and received plenty of good influence from those ancient religions. Thus those old teachers have been with us as our guardian angels in our life; they themselves or their representatives. – And in this life the best in our souls has been that which we had learned in the previous life.

When we have lived in Christendom we have received influences from a new teacher: Jesus Christ. Although it is common – excluding modern theosophy – that in this visible life man receives some influences from Jesus Christ but the ethical basis he receives, the one that is provided us in the modern Christendom is the ethic of Moses. – I wish to say no ill about Moses, but merely to state that we take very little from Jesus Christ here in the Christendom.

When we die, the moral force that has purified us in the purgatory has come from Moses. It is as if he had stood there and thrown us into a cauldron of purification. But when we enter our earliest childhood and birth we meet our past teachers Buddha and Confucius, and they tell us of Christ, they remind us what we have heard about him in the visible life. And we move towards that heaven where Jesus Christ is. We know that the cosmic mystic Christ is in every teacher, but then we enter the domain of Jesus Christ, we enter heaven. And we feel that this is all very peculiar; we start to shiver in our soul, even though we are already purified. If we have been religious on Earth, belonged to a specific church, then in the final state we are at first with the people and teachers who have told us about Christ. But then when we also meet those other teachers we find out in our soul that we have not know what Christ is, we have not heard properly about Christ. Everything becomes translucent to us, the whole theology is forgotten and we know we are approaching a great, wonderful reality which we cannot really understand. Then open up the gates to the real heaven where only our higher selves exist. We die to our personality and feel as if we must plunge into an abyss or fly over one, although we cannot do it; but that we must do. And we feel that in that abyss there is infinite agony and solitude and we fall into it. And then man as a soul plunges into that abyss, into unspeakable agony, just as he has been fearing with a shivering premonition. But at the same time he notices, knows and feels that this agony is the door to the greatest joy. For ordinary people it is very difficult to imagine those heavenly experiences.

The life he lives in heaven is comparable to our waking life here but without all the realistic images. It is not pondering over the impression derived from our daily life, but instead it is an overwhelming fulfilment and fruition of all the good and beautiful and sublime that was in us in the earthly life. That is why it is heaven. It is the result of the effects, the teachings of the nightly life. It is exactly the same when a person wakes up in the morning from a refreshing sleep and feels like a new person filled with energy to do good. It is as if his life in heaven were permeated with that kind of mood that is made up of all the most sacred moments of the waking life. This last period in the afterlife is Sun-life, it is pure brightness and only the most high, most sacred and best can flourish and endure in it.

It is impossible for a man to withstand it for long for it is only purest of emotion. He feels that he must return once more to the school of life experiences. And he descends into a fog and sees before him his future life, how he will experience a lot and aspire hard in those experiences, and how he must become good, wise and pure. And he feels joy watching that extraordinary opportunity that is offered. And then he promises to life: "I want to try my best in my next life, I want to remember that it is a school. I want to forget myself and work for others." And he promises this in joy and begins to descend into the world; and a new personality will begin to form.

And the teacher, let us say Moses, who was of great importance to him in his previous life, – and to some extent Jesus –, will prepare him for his new incarnation.

XII
THE UNDERWORLD

When the giant steamship Titanic approached the coast of America just before the First World War it struck an iceberg and started to sink. All the thousands of people travelling in it knew that the possibilities to be saved were slim, and that most people would face death. – It is said that at that gravest of moments the ship's orchestra started to play the so-called hymn of the Titanic: "Nearer, My God, To Thee." People were able to control their emotions and be prepared to cross the final frontier; and their only solace being that they might get closer to God.

This idea that in death man approaches God is not unfounded. It is the correct idea, although we know there can be a great deal of suffering after death, so we might ask how do we, by entering hell, come closer to God. However it is so that the whole life after death is about getting closer to God and the great truth of life. To those remarks I made in the previous chapter I would like to add that death, even as it has been called the highest and most solemn of events of this visible life, is so sublime, so wonderful and joyous, because it takes us closer to the living truth of life, God.

I would like to depict the life after death from the point of view of dead people. We have done this many times earlier and I do not claim that I would have anything principally new now; but there might be some points of view that have not been emphasized so much. I think this depiction of the post mortem life from the viewpoint of the dead is important because it would confirm the description given in theosophical and antroposophical literature.

As we recall Madame Helena Blavatsky and the masters did not at first speak much about post mortem life, at least not of the astral side of the afterlife; they emphasized that the real place for afterlife is heaven which is the most important aspect of afterlife. Perhaps they wanted to refer to the fact that when we as disciples wish to follow in master's footsteps and attain some personal knowledge of these things, then the after world and the experiences of a human soul in the purgatory are the most accessible to us; they become clear in a bright and clear light. Life in heaven on the other hand is more difficult to examine because of its great brightness. When a disciple has entered the afterlife and studied its phenomena it is easy for him to understand the astral world in afterlife; i.e. those phenomena which follow this (present) physical, bodily life before the human soul arrives in heaven. Maybe Madame Blavatsky and the masters wished to emphasize somewhat that these are matters that can be found out about on your own. We wish to emphasize only the point that one should not take so-called spiritualistic announcements literally. In séances there comes up much information about the afterlife, for the dead reveal it. But if we take these things literally as they come from the medium and view them as something higher than this physical life is, then we miss the right proportion and perspective to things, for these phenomena must not be studied from below but from above. Madame Blavatsky emphasized in her writings to esoterists that they must be studied so that a man as if from heaven above enters the after world below. Then the after death conditions are seen in their proper perspective. This is of extreme importance, for otherwise, when closing on the Moon, we might become enraptured by the phenomena of the afterlife, especially in their highest form. They could be seen in such wonderful light that we would not understand why we should be here in the physical plane in the first place. Living there would be much better. This thought would be so natural to a man that he would want voluntarily to resign his physical life. This is obviously a wrong outlook for then everyone would want to end their lives. Therefore it is important that the post mortem phenomena in the after world are studied from above, from heaven, so that we would get the right perspective. Anyhow, when we take the viewpoint of the dead, as we wish to do now, we must inevitably use a language known to us in this physical life and depict the phenomena with it, so that we would understand them. Thus the depictions may get a slightly materialistic tinge. But when we remember that our language in this world is inadequate, that we can but one-sidedly depict the phenomena of the invisible world, then we will not fall into the delusion that it would portray the truth in its entirety.

In the last chapter I tried to describe the whole of the after world from a theoretic-objective perspective and portray its phenomena from a comprehensive point of view and their relationship to this everyday life here. But now, so that the description would not be left too general without any personally vibrant life, I wish to portray it from the viewpoint of the dead and hope that you would remember all the aforementioned details.

It is said of the post mortem life that it is remembering of and going through backwards the earthly life all the way to birth and the post mortem phases of the preceding life. This is a general depiction but in reality it is not so simple, but instead it is living experiencing, which is as if summarized, for after world has different grades and we move from grade to grade, from lower to upper depending on what everyone is in their souls. What is animal in his soul will come forth there. Not everyone attends every grade; it depends on their level of inner development. There might be good people who at first are at a very low grade but move on very quickly to a very high grade; such has their life been. They have had a distinct vice that first needed to be purified. On the other hand there are people who spend long times on lower grade and very little time on an upper. – In theosophical literature these are called the *seven sublevels*.

Each person must pass through post mortem life, but the less selfishness and personal weaknesses one has had in his life the faster he progresses through these planes nearer to the Moon and enters the Sun.

When we take a look at the different sublevels of the after world and start from the lowest in the underworld, we see that as the theosophical literature tells us, there are the people who have strong sensual desires. The people who keep eating or drinking as their god or sexual life as their highest to be worshipped, as well as all animal desires one can name. Also all violent people and murderers are on the lowest grade in the afterlife. – What is especially difficult for the person wanting to study these things is that he does not seem to be in contact with human beings; he does not see real humans in this lower world. This level is rather dark, a murky place with thick air; here one is dealing with some kind of animals who are not strictly animals, but some kind of monsters with distorted, horrid faces; but otherwise they somehow resemble humans. It's hard to watch their unspeakable agonies; a burning fire lives in them, for all the lusts they had during their lives exist now as their coarsest body. In other words: they lack the physical body with which to cover these desires as they did in the physical life. – People think that the desires live in the physical body and can even torment it when they begin to work on themselves, but they forget that the body is a temple of the Holy Spirit. There is an animal in man that is vestige from the animalistic time and which he has been nourishing. It dwells within us, full of lust and desire, but is not the physical body itself. With the body we only satiate the lust temporarily. Everyone knows that lust can be sated only temporarily; hunger and thirst emerge yet again. Nothing ever becomes satiated with the body but the desire grows ever stronger. In this visible world man's only solace is to be momentarily sated and for a while be at peace. But in death he faces the great reality; he has desires but he cannot satisfy them. There he cannot manifest the desires through the physical organism for he has none, so the desires in his consciousness are savagely fierce and mesmerizing. He has no other thoughts than satisfying his desires. When we observe these beings in the astral world we understand that it is natural for those wretched souls to instinctually seek the company of people in such places on Earth where such desires are sated. If a person goes drinking he is not alone, but he is attacked by a swarm of invisible savage beings who cry within him: "Oh, satisfy us too!" He is not consumed only by his own lust but also by the lust of the dead souls; and they all beg for satisfaction through him. Of course their satisfaction is minimal because it comes through another person, and therefore they are in constant agony. It depends on how strong this desire is, and how long it lasts, – until the deceased understands that it is impossible to satiate. Upon noticing this they feel that all the organs used to satisfy these lusts are non-existent; the mouth that is like an animal's mouth becomes sick and falls off and they become absolutely miserable. At the same time they tell themselves: this is horrible, I am in hell; there is no other way to escape than to get rid of these desires and wants. Of course there are helpers present who tell them that they are not in eternal torment. At first they do not listen but laugh the laugh which always echoes in hell; but eventually they will listen to the voice of the helper. Finally they understand that as it is impossible to satisfy any desires it is better to give them up. Also at the same time the seriousness of life becomes clear to many a soul. Many souls have been received there with the explanation: you are dying, you cannot step before God as such animals; you must be purified and then face God. Many understand this and for them it is relatively easy to get rid of their desires, and they feel their self fading away. It is exactly the same phenomenon as with the physical body. When a person departs his physical body it dissolves; it turns into atoms in death and rejoins the cosmic life. – In passing we can say that especially in Egypt this dissolution was tried to avoid, for as long as the physical body remains the etheric body remains as well. And as long one has an etheric body one need not turn into an animal but he can retain his former shape, and with the etheric body he can exist among humans and wander here on Earth. He remains human even though he cannot partake in any human activities or be seen by others. The ghastly states of loneliness involved in that the Egyptians tried to avoid with magic. This was a very bold attempt. On the other hand it is good, but on the other hand it is black magic for it tries to prevent the normal circle of life and control how the afterlife should be; as if karma and divine forces would not know better how things should be. Therefore on my behalf I cannot approve this old Egyptian way, although it may be that many of us have been involved in this; to me now it appears to be black magic.

When we move from the lowest grade to the next higher one we see how in the second grade there already are decent human souls. They are no longer animals. They are men but they think that the only charm in life, if not its purpose, is to have something sensually titillating in order to keep interested in this physical world. For example, there are men regarded totally decent by the world who in marital life hold sex in such a high regard that it gives them strength and courage to live. To them this physical life is so hard without it. They focus their entire attention on it and think that it is their only joy in life. I, no more than nature, wish to judge nothing but experience tells that this is unwise; for in the other world, on the second grade of the after world are those souls to whom such sensual satisfaction is very important, the personal joy in life, and they continue it there.

Therefore often in séances we get a message from the dead that all is well, for: "The first moment I got here I met my wife and I'm happy." If we ask "Do you carry on your sexual life like on Earth? Is there no difference?" They reply: – "There is the difference that we have no children." – But in fact they slightly exaggerate their joy, for when observing this from above we notice how they themselves are wondering. They are not very happy, they feel no particular satisfaction. It is strange to them; they may discuss how they cannot bear children like on Earth. And they begin to feel that this kind of sexual life is meaningless. As long as it has a purpose it is attractive, but when it starts to feel a bit empty it puzzles them and finally they see that they are in a different world and one is not supposed to be there like on Earth.

Therefore part in the after world is a good lesson to us showing that in reality no natural instinct, such as sexuality can satisfy anybody forever unless one sees a meaningful purpose in it. I mentioned this as a small example although I could talk about the many different sides of it, but this example is good enough to describe the conditions there.

When we move on to the third grade we meet souls with such experiences that they had regarded the physical life beautiful because it has so orderly and neat patterns and habits. We eat and drink and work in the office, in the fields etc., we go to bed, sleep and wake up again to drink coffee and eat. All this regularity is in its own way charming and to many people it becomes the meaning of life, so that other subjects, like spirituality are left aside. All those patterns feel much more real; as if that were the only real life. Spiritual life is left for Sundays. This is so natural in the visible life that only in the afterlife we finally notice that it is charming for a while, but then we start wondering why nothing really satisfies us. We sleep, wake up and are not refreshed; and there is no real appetite even when faced with lovely fruits and champagne; when one eats and drinks he is not sated. The ancient Greeks described this so that when the dead were offered delicacies, grapes, etc. they tried to grasp them to no avail, for they could not get hold of anything. It is a metaphor. And so it is that when the dead person pours for himself the proper amount of wine he is accustomed to and drinks, he will get no satisfaction. And when he eats he will also get no satisfaction. They do get aid from helpers who explain that they are in a different world in which everything must be taken differently. All routines will begin to seem pointless, all doings meaningless. A person who imagines himself to be in his office does not really get a grasp of the situation. What is all this? He wants to find out about everything and what is the purpose of this. He is amazed by everything until he meets a helper who says to him: "You are not on Earth, but in heaven."

When we move even higher to the fourth grade we meet people who in life have had the idea that this physical life is the only real and important one. It is like some Mephistopheles were whispering in our ear that this physical life is the only real life; in this we must work and live. If this attitude results in something beautiful, good and cultivating in life, then it is called for; but if there's any of the feeling that this is the only reality of which we can know about, then it will be confront us on the fourth grade. It is the final touchstone to our practical materialism. Therefore there end all the souls who in practical terms are materialists, even unbeknownst to themselves, and who theoretically and philosophically think that this physical life is the only reality. – Therefore, in their emphasis on this life, some people commit all sorts of crimes: they leave the country after embezzling the cash register, forge bills etc. This is not only the result of moral deficiency but also that of practical materialism: if he cannot gather enough with work then he must steal and counterfeit. This is particularly a phenomenon of the modern world and we should not judge people too harshly, for their behaviour derives from desperation in their souls. Their souls are upset; they want money and so they will do anything to be able to "live large". Only after death, or perhaps earlier, they clearly see how futile it is to sell something as valuable as their soul for something as worthless as money gained by wrong means. Upon noticing this they become angry with themselves. – Usually on the fourth grade people understand the reality of the physical life is not in forms, although they do not yet understand where the reality is. Only a profoundly moral person of occultist persuasion can understand where this reality lies. Here there can be found true hard working men and rather moral and fine people who have believed that this physical life is exactly real in its external forms. In afterlife they notice that the physical type of living as if fades away from their hands and they cannot hold on to it; everything vanishes into thin air even though they have believed it so real.

Of course something is always left of a person for he is able to move to a higher grade in the after world: the fifth grade where is found everything artistic, scientific and inventive. In general the life in which one exerts his brain, as in all scientific creative work – not only his hands. In this fifth world he will see what is real and what is not; for if he, strangely enough, happens to be in his scientific or artistic work charmed by the formal side of his work he will be sorely tested. – I remember well being young and indecisive whether to accept this society as such and serve it or not. I thought that if society understands me I would be very grateful to it and would willingly serve it, but if not, I would rather go my own way and try to do something useful without the approval of society. I had applied for a substantial scholarship from the university and was thinking of going abroad. With the application I sent a clarification of what I intended to research: it included spiritism, hypnotism, etc. I thought that if the university understood this and would grant me the scholarship I would be very grateful. Then the whole civilized world would have shown its approval and proved that for it too is the puzzle of death important. And then I would have wanted to show my gratitude by becoming a professor in our university. When I had sent the application I started to write my doctorial thesis "Vägen til Kunskapen" ("The way to knowledge"). I sat in my room and had great tomes before me which I had collected from the university's library. Some of them were truly ancient; one of them had a text in Sanskrit; that I would have translated and annotated and thus explained the path to knowledge. But while doing that work I made a psychological observation: I started to enjoy having such great, thick tomes before me which I would browse and leaf through, or just watch them. I thought that this was a wonderful life; if one could live in such a way here on Earth then life would be enjoyable and wonderful.

At that same time I was undergoing an inner training, which I mentioned in my book "Tieni totuuden lähteelle" ("My path to the source of truth"). I had investigated the afterlife – this was in 1890's – and started to wonder where my enjoyment of the research would take me. So I took the issue with me to the after world and observed what kind of effects it would have. Then I noticed how for many a scientist the scientific research could become so attractive, even a pleasure, so that it bound him to a specific grade of the underworld. I was horrified and thought it better that the university not give me a scholarship – and if it did I would have to be very careful. Everything ended up well, for no such scholarship was granted to me. Naturally they did not take me seriously. On the contrary, it was ridiculed in the newspapers; and this ridicule was a good educational experience for me. I realized in what kind of temptations we as spiritual beings might end up in this visible life. It is so with all artistic and scientific work, that not only is the work attractive, but that another factor can become very fateful in the afterlife; and that is when we are working for fame and glory. But then we can ask whether those artists, poets, authors etc. are not very rare who do not do their work for personal glory? – The more they think about their own glory the more they bind themselves to the school of the after world.

I remember an experience about this in the after world. I met a poet there. When I came to him he was very polite and bade me welcome to his house; he had a very beautiful mansion which he had built himself. He introduced me his home and told me he led an especially happy life there. I noticed that he had not yet realized that he was dead. When he then took me to his house, his beautiful and splendid mansion, I gazed upwards and noticed that the ceiling in the great hall was like the dome in a church; it had many paintings in the walls and doors and openings to other rooms. But when we were about to leave the hall and enter one room I noticed it did not have a floor, and he said: "Be careful, everything is not quite ready yet."And when I watched more closely I noticed the floor was made of dirt and there was filled with moss and mire and water, and perhaps there were even lizards and snakes; everything was green, dirty and black. – He had acquired some lamps, and he asked me to another room which was none the better than the previous one. He had received me outside with such a great and dignified way, as if to say: "Look, how wonderful!", – and I had been full of gratefulness towards him. But then he suddenly changed and there was not a hint left of pride and splendour; he was just ashamed. Then I understood how matters were and explained a little what was going on. It was hard; and he noticed that one has to give up personal glory, as well as the pursuit of it. – I was taught the lesson that in this visible life it is safe and necessary to give up glory and take life seriously, if we wish to journey to God.

On the sixth grade we see only good people who have worked only for the common good and for the best of all men, great philanthropists, inventors and other scientists; different kinds of benefactors who have tried to do something for the benefit of mankind. We notice that if they have had any personal interest and if the so called sacrifice and helping of others has been such that it brought enjoyment and glory, it has bound them to these experiences in the afterlife on the sixth grade. And their experience is that they see what they are building: it is as if they were building castles in the air. They watch mankind and people and realize that everything they do for helping and sacrifice is in vain, until they find out that the only good in their work is that which brings no pleasure or glory; only that remains. This is an excellent psychological observation!

On the seventh grade of the after world we notice if we in our lifetime have emphasized our own personal soul life, if our own feelings and thoughts have been important and real to us, in the same manner will our interest be in our own soul life in the after world. – Many religious people think that we must make ourselves better, and so it is for everyone who strives forward. It feels natural but yet it is an illusion. In the after world one will see that all this emphasizing of one's self is but fading fog. We must give up that as well.

We may now consider that we have gone through all the sublevels of the after world, and it is as if everything had grown larger grade by grade. In the end we feel as if our personality should fade away so that we would not exist at all. But at the same time something else begins to loom in the distance. Somewhere deep something looms bright, something we barely dare to believe in but in which we have to start believing. When we arrive at the gates of heaven we come so naked that there is not a trace left of our personality. In a sense it is all like a tragedy, but at the same time there lies the great promise: "Man, you are approaching God, the truth of life. Fear not that you have to give up yourself, for those who do so, attain to the great truth of their life." – In the afterlife all this will begin to become clear to us; and in the after world we eventually end up as if in space, in emptiness – and then we knock on the gates of heaven.

XIII
HEAVEN

Everyone really knows intuitively what is the meaning of life. Of course not everyone formulates it philosophically nor answers the question in the same words, but everyone knows the answer within himself. Perhaps people in their youth have a hunch of the general idea and then when older know more in detail what their life's purpose is. For to every man has been set this question of his life's purpose. – If we set the question in a broad, general way, for example, what is the purpose of existence, then we might get a more or less competent philosophical answer. But it is harder then to come up with an answer that would satisfy all so that they could accept it within. For example, it is said that the purpose of human life is to become perfect. But when people get older they feel that they cannot become perfect humans, so they find this answer vague and too general to be satisfying, although they admit the truth in it. But when the question "What is the purpose and goal of life" is set as a personal question so that everyone asks "What is the purpose of my life?", then echoes a voice in young as well as old: "You must get rid of your weaknesses." A person is not satisfied with himself as long as he sees flaws and weaknesses in him which he deems unworthy and which have no value. Every person feels when young as well as old: "I have my weaknesses; I must get rid of them." Or he knows the answer to that question in a different way.

151

A voice echoes within him which tells him: "You must do this in life; you have been given your job; perform it well." And while living in the world one has a peaceful conscience and can accept one's self to the extent he performs the task he has been given. He feels that he has a particular artistic, scientific or practical work to do and feels within that if he is loyal to this work, if he does his best and tries to be even better than his best then is his conscience peaceful. And he feels: "This is the purpose of my life." He demands the greatest perfection from himself in his job. And if one feels there are flaws and weaknesses in one's character, he demands the same perfection in relation to them as well.

Like this every person knows within him what is the purpose of life; otherwise he would not have the strength to live. If we do not live only for pleasure and amusement, but long for a life with reason as well, then we get a satisfactory answer to the question of the meaning and purpose of life. And when we are in this way loyal to our personal life we understand that the human life has been set a much higher destination than our personal life. One of its names is human perfection and to that all of us human beings must strive for; we must attain perfection. Of course that feels distant and unattainable, something we can believe in but cannot in practical terms think that we could reach such perfection.

This feeling we have of the purpose of life is based on the natural fact that existence, life, is arranged as a school, as we like to say. Life is a great kindergarten, school and university and academy which everyone attends. Naturally most people do not believe any of such things in their waking consciousness but say: "How could one achieve anything in this one life? A person does not live after death; that is fantasy, imagination and not scientifically real." Many people think this way. And therefore it is very wonderful to look upon life as a school, to watch the history of human souls, to watch their journey in this visible life and then in the so-called invisible life. For then, when we observe the history of a human soul we notice that every soul learns to see, every personality learns to know what is the meaning of life; if not in the visible life then in the invisible one. For it is as if every personality had been given a task to labour for a certain perfection. Every time a human soul is born into this world and a new personality is formed, it is as if in the field of that latent personality were sown a seed containing as a promising, wonderful ideal the full blossoming into perfection of that personality. When a person is born into the world he hides within himself a seed. This seed contains the seed of his own perfection; it is the seed for the flower which he must blossom into. And because it is determined by fate, because this seed is planted in the field of the human soul one cannot avoid it; he cannot avoid becoming this flower which is hidden in his soul. And if he will not become that in this visible life, he will become it after death. Therefore we can say that every personality reaches its own perfection, and will reach it after death if not in this world. For the life after death is the continuation, and we might add, mandatory continuation, of this life in the direction that is destined, and which a man has possibly tried to avoid in his visible life. A person might have said: "I am not bothered to work on my personality, and to complete such a task I imagined for myself when I was young." – Nature will not prevent him from saying so, but nature says to him when he dies:" Now you must in any case reach the perfection you have been appointed. You must become so pure, so bright you could have become while living; now you must do the work that you could have for the most part fulfilled while living." In this sense nature is totally relentless. In this sense existence is no child's play, it is no game. Often times a person ignores these thoughts and says: "I will see it when I die; and I wonder if there even is a life after death."– And after death one will see that life, existence is more serious than what he thought, more magical and beautiful than he could have ever imagined. So many people are pessimistic in life and see everything as sordid, ugly: "All people are selfish; everything is based on cruelty; people are like wolves amongst each other who eat one another; this life is anything but noble and beautiful!"

In such a pessimistic way people think often times. We need not go any further than the daily conditions to see that people are often miserable in their family lives, they argue, they are unable to reach happiness and contentment. They all walk alone in their agony and feel that there is no understanding, no brotherhood nor happiness – everything is so hard. These earthly conditions are so very difficult; we must work to make a living; and often we are even denied the possibility of work so that one may even have to go hungry; he cannot even feed his own children. The social conditions are so inadequate. Life can be so hard in this visible life that a person may think: "Who is behind all this? It must be evil as the source of all." – But then after death he will have experiences that show and prove him that existence is basically wonderful and beautiful, so noble and sublime that could not believe it when living; it goes beyond his understanding how it is possible that existence is so unspeakably wondrous. But in the end we can, as logical thinkers arrive to a conclusion and ask, how could we even think that life itself, that is one and behind everything could be evil, could be inharmonious. There could not be anything, there could not be absolute existence if it were not unconditional bliss and peace.

This we can understand logically, but practically it is harder because the solar system, and this Earth as well, is a hard school.

When a person dies he must become perfect; he must reach the perfection he was decreed as a personal being. When a person dies he comes closer to God. Death is journeying to God. Death is, as we said in the previous chapter, first a journey to the Moon and then to the Sun. And we can say: Life after death is the same as if a person would take the path of purification to the school of initiation. Here on Earth people are offered, and have always been offered, a chance to take the path of purification towards initiation. In all religions, in every occult school people have been told: "Purify yourselves, take your destined path which we show you and you shall become initiated, you will enter the brotherhood, the kingdom of heaven. For in its deepest meaning this life is a school. If you understand this and willingly travel alongside nature, and help nature, you will with your own efforts and of your free own will achieve that which you must mandatorily achieve after death." After death it is mandatory for man to take the path of purification to initiation and become initiated into the universal brotherhood. But because it is mandatory, because it is dictated by nature, it does not really matter much whether man himself wants it or not. It is more like a tragedy, as if a proof – I mean regarding eternal life – that we have neglected much of what we could have accomplished – which we did not want to understand. Therefore it does not matter so much. For when man is reincarnated on Earth that what he has previously gone through in his afterlife is like a seed within him, but it will not bloom in his lifetime unless he wants it. This life is the essential time, as Jesus said, this is the period when we must make a choice, a change of heart. Here man must willingly do good, love the truth. This will happen after death, but because then it happens perforce man will not gain merit from it; only negative merit, the merit of suffering. Even if he has achieved initiation after death he will not be an initiated person when he is born again here – unless he has achieved it in his previous personality on Earth.

This is a very fascinating and curious observation one can make regarding life after death. And the reason for it is that our solar system is arranged as a school. The planets with their beings represent certain attainments, certain qualities, virtues, and influence each other by emitting each a powerful effect and a spiritual current to the others. There is also a physical effect but foremost of all it is an invisible, spiritual current. We, being here on Earth are influenced strongly by Mercury and Venus, as well as the ones further away: Neptune, Uranus etc. We receive from them psychological, psychic currents. And all those currents expose the beings here, especially the humans, to special specific influences, to school. And because Mercury and

Venus are closest to Earth they were allowed in the dawn of time to send here helpers and teachers, who formed the original occult academy; the teachers who work invisibly among people. The task of the teachers is to affect people in a purifying manner, to uplift them so that they could reach the initiation belonging here on Earth. Therefore the power current of Venus-Mercury, when occultly observing, is a purifying one. And the teachers who came from there told the weak beings of Earth: "Give up sin, change your ways!" – All religions have taught so; and secret schools have organized certain training through which man must travel to purification. But during the ages relatively few people in this visible life have listened to the voice of the teachers. – Although altogether there might be great many of them – even a hundred thousand – ,but regarding how many souls belong to Earth, it is a tiny number of people who have listened to the teachers and started purifying themselves. Thus people usually come under the influence of Venus-Mercury when they have died. And when a person after death comes under the strong influence of Venus-Mercury, its strong currents of fire train him and purify his soul, so that in the afterword he will first travel to the Moon and from there to the Sun. So for example here in the Christendom one may meet Moses when he faces death. It means that in that case to him Moses represents the moral in the so-called ten commandments of God, which he has known and approved in his waking consciousness, which have been taught to him and which he has broken. Moses is as if his judge; to put it in another way, the fiery current from Mercury-Venus that faces him in the astral plane is the judge and executor of all the commands of Moses, and demands: "You must fulfill all of God's Ten Commandments. For what you have broken you shall be purified of after death." An Indian deceased faces a rishi, a sage, a Zoroastrian faces Zoroaster, a Buddhist faces the Buddha. Each will face the morality he has learned to accept in the visible world. If he has not followed it, it will face him in the after world and say: "Now you must purify yourself, so you can say like it is said in the Egyptian Book of the Dead: 'I have no sins, I have not stolen, or murdered, have not made a false oath, I have not done this or that.' – In the Egyptian formula the deceased lists all kinds of sins and weaknesses he has not done, or which he has purified himself. If he has committed sins while on Earth he must have purged himself of them in the purgatory. Only then has he accomplished his after world journey to the Moon, and in the Moon he will face his teacher personally; and only then will the gates of heaven open.

If we would describe the life after death in musically, we would say it is a melody, it is melodies: in the Moon man is alone and shouts out his agony. Human souls possessed by common lust rage like madmen. Everyone is alone, fighting their own demons, fighting against their own sins. Therefore is the hardest part in hell and purgatory the loneliness, the fact that one feels himself abandoned even by God. A human soul will feel this more or less strongly. Those who are a bit stronger themselves may feel this even too tragically. – In this life as well it is the tragedy of all great men. The hardest thing we can face in this visible life is that no one cares about us, no one will take our tired head in their lap, that no one will wipe away our tears. When we feel ourselves thus rejected in this physical life, it is true agony; it is the hardest thing of all, the deepest suffering. – And let it be stated in passing: Every occultist must pass through this experience over and over again, until it does not frighten him, until he fills it with brightness. – The undercurrent of hell and purgatory is precisely this feeling of loneliness, and it must be overcome, for life slips away from your hands, your self fades into non-existence; even if man would scream all he could he would have nothing left but the melody he himself is.

On the other hand, life in heaven is exactly the opposite. In musical terms we could say the life in heaven is harmony, because different melodies blend in each other harmoniously there. For our only real happiness is that we feel our connection with others. – That is the only happiness

157

in family life as well, that everybody loves and trusts each other; everyone feels they could die for the others; no one asks anything else than being able to love. That is how it is in a happy family. When two people love each other and form a family, their love is in that they trust each other, that they need not suspect each other; they know that they will work for a shared home; they feel that they have a mutual ideal for which they wish to live for. That is heaven. Heaven is in a multitude of people together who can form a harmonious whole, ready to live and die for each other, for a beautiful cause. – Even a war troop going to battle and death when commanded is like an earthly reflection of something heavenly. Their great love for their commander, their willingness to give their lives, their great love for their fatherland for which they are willing to die, there is a reflection of heavenly unity. In times past this could be unspeakably idealistic, sublime and beautiful. Now we perhaps do not think so of armed forces; we no longer have such wars on Earth, at least not in the modern cultures. Now it is more like infinite hell with glimpses of heaven when opposing soldiers are reconciled, when dying together the enemies realise: "We are all brothers". For a moment, there is heaven. In modern wars and armies there no longer is any heavenly dimension because not even the soldiers always know what are they fighting for. They might think now: If those statesmen and rulers had not argued we would not have been sent into such misery either. But there might be a glimpse of heaven even in this, for there is a glimpse of heaven in every circumstance of life, in prisons, in the worst pits of sin; everywhere there is the divine heaven, but only in momentarily glimpses. – For heaven itself, the real heaven we experience after death, is in harmony and unity. Heaven would not be happiness and beatitude if it were not togetherness with many others. It is not that one would be united with strangers – this happens to only a few – ,but one is together with people he has always loved, always known, the ones he had wanted to be good to, and the ones he had wanted to love. With all these souls one ends up together in wondrous harmony, for they all love him.

If a person while living on Earth had grieved deeply that someone whom he had loved had not understood him, has things differently in heaven. The key to heaven is love; love opens the gates of heaven, nothing else but love, love for people, for ideas, for God, for all beings. Love is the key that opens up heaven. Therefore it has been said: When entering heaven man carries a as if vase in his hand, – some smaller, some really big – and everyone's vase is filled to with heavenly flowers. It is the vase of happiness. As much as a person can be beatific and happy in a spiritual way so much he will receive in heaven. One who can love more carries a larger vase, one who can love less carries a smaller vase – but in heaven everyone's love will reach such a peak that he cannot wish for any more, even if that love were limited to just two or three persons or an idea. In heaven he can give this love from himself.

But we ask with all due reason: is life in heaven spent in vain, is it spent on personal happiness? Is there no use for life in heaven; is there no work done? And the answer is: Life in heaven is not in vain but it is of great importance; it is a great preparation, it is great work. For what is life in heaven? We just said that from the point of view of eternal life it is attaining initiation after the path of purification. And initiation is in reality that a person is spiritually united with a few or very many souls, with whom he can experience the beatitude and happiness of life; but at the same time it is an initiation to the actual school. If a person here takes the path of purification and becomes initiated into the White Brotherhood then will his true school begin. And so it is after death as well. When a person enters into unity and harmony with other souls, so that they sing together beautiful polyphonic choral or play a symphony; then also will he enter a school. – So life in heaven is stepping away from the moon and its influence, and moving into the Sun and the sphere of influence that consists of the further planets: in heaven we come in contact with Mars, Jupiter and Saturn. It is like a wonderful journey out into space.

There is no more suffering in us, no weakness, no sin; we as personalities are as we could have been if we could have kept in our hearts the image of God, that flower we originally had there. We are then angelic beings; not very wise because we never were wise personalities, but pure, childlike personalities – like children going dancing and playing. But we are not going dancing and playing, we are going to school. And the nearest school people end up in the life in heaven is the school of Mars, the occult influence of Mars. This is naturally figurative speech; it is not to be taken materialistically. Some go on to the schools of Jupiter and Saturn, very few in the schools of Uranus and Neptune. At the least 99%, we could say even 99,99% are limited to the school of Mars. And what is this school of Mars, this wondrous heavenly school we end up after death in heaven? Those who have read my book "Tähtikoulut" ("Astral Schools"), remember that the school of Mars is said to be the school and planet of soldiers; and also the initiatory school of the red fire. The school of Mars is that in which everyone goes through in heaven, in which the human souls clearly see that one must not argue, not wage war, must not force, not use violence, and not be evil. Everything that to us here on Earth is casual and commonplace, is put into a bright spotlight in heaven under the influence of Mars. Not in a way that it would arouse any difficult feelings or suffering within us; not so for we no longer see earthly conditions, we no longer understand anything else than inability to argue, wage war, wield a sword or any weapon, resort to violence at all. We know that; we live in such consciousness that no evil can be done. In such clear consciousness we live in heaven. And therefore our souls resound together in harmony. In Mars-heaven souls divide themselves into groups according to how many other souls they love and know, and they form their own spheres; and each group has their own tune, their harmonious symphony, and together they form a tune in a greater whole, or a song which they sing. One choir could sing: "Oh, how happy is the family in which rules a harmony between man and wife and children", and another: "Oh, how happy is the religious community who wishes to do good to the whole of mankind and love everybody." The message of the third choir could be: "How happy is the society that wants to serve people, that wishes best for everyone." And large masses feel together: "What happiness it is when all men have good will and there is peace on Earth." And large masses also feel that: "The only real content in life is that we sing praise to God in heaven."

And where are these souls? They are in space, within the sphere of our Sun, – and the sun contains the whole solar system in it. The human souls from Earth are not bound to any location. Souls in heaven, who journey to the planets, are at the same time here in our conscience and hearts. That is their field of work. They sing to us harmony, peace and love. Therefore we can notice how in religions the dead have been revered and thought of with love; how people on Earth have turned to their ancestors and said: "You, who are in heaven, look upon me so that I may have peace." And people who quarrel with other might think: "I wonder what my relative, the dear departed might think if he would look at me?" – People have an instinctual knowledge of the dead in heaven constantly sing peace and praise to God. Therefore it is said in religions that the angels sing. They are the dead – and also many other beings. Angels who are not human number in millions and millions. One such angel leads the heavenly choir; and that is real work. As a reflection of that we have melodies and music on Earth. We might think that singing and playing is just for amusement's sake. No, it is work; it is enlightening work for the good of men, for when it is singed and music is played it makes the human souls vibrate. It is work, and it comes from heaven. – What else matters than human souls growing closer to God, becoming more divine, more like the heavenly Father. It matters not what we have accomplished; everything we do on Earth is so little, just like walking by the sea and picking up colourful little stones. Even a great poet thinks like that of his work when he has felt in his soul what monumental work is done in space; he has had a glimpse of those millions and billions of souls who work in the school in which souls are growing. Therefore this work is the most important of all. What we do in our own personality is very small; it is the growing of our own flower so that we would be faithful to ourselves as well. The world is not overturned by that. The great forces of the world put us into school so that we can try to be faithful to ourselves. The greatest harmony in the world is formed from the song of billions of souls which resounds in space. And when a man becomes self-aware, when he can hear the music which has resounded deep in his soul since the dawn of time, then a new life will begin for him.

Only a few people move from the influence of Mars to the influence of Jupiter, for the influence of Jupiter is not negative, as is the matter with Mars, which is positive only in such a way that it gives something in the place of the negative. The influence of Jupiter is positive. One who goes into that school after death comes under the influence in which he learns and becomes used to sowing good things. We could say metaphorically: Under the influence of Jupiter man digs up a diamond, or several, from the ground and knows that he must give them to others. He feels he possesses a great wealth and is obliged to give from it to others; and he wonders that his wealth just keeps on growing; if he gives away one jewel he has ten left, if he donates one diamond he has a thousand in its place.

Such is the influence of Jupiter. We need not to try and describe it any more for, like it was said, only a few souls are there. "Many are called, few are chosen." – Even fewer are under the influence of Saturn when they have died, for it is as if man learned to create, to build a temple. He is like a stone, a burning stone; he ignites other stones and builds a temple. He is a creator. We cannot describe it with words. And what comes to Uranus and Neptune we have not needed yet their heavens in life after death. Their influence comes through Mars and Venus. We have enough schooling with the others in our life in heaven.

One peculiar matter in life after death is that after the work of Jesus Christ he, Christ himself, is at the threshold of death in the afterlife. But only very few people can yet plead to him, for only those who have already followed him here on Earth can come to Jesus Christ, – and not in any indefinite way so that they would have heard about him but have not known his commandments and counsel. Not in that way for it may be that one who thinks he is following Christ tries to follow some other morality and ends up under the influence of, for example, Moses. Only those who try to follow the commandments of Jesus, and in that way follow him, will meet the true Jesus after death. Their hell and purgatory, if they have to go through them, are peculiar in a sense that through all the hardships and agonies Jesus Christ shines as a wonderful forgiving force; so that even in the purgatory one may become aware that it is not only suffering that purifies and teaches and delivers him from plight, but that there is also a beckoning force of love which lets the suffering pass quickly and in a way that the soul can overcome it by itself. I cannot find the right words to describe this but let us say this: a person is in a grave plight; he is enveloped in a predicament; he is as if in prison and cannot escape; he just suffers in agony and he has the feeling inside him that he should suffer. The kind of person who has followed Jesus does not complain about anything, is not dissatisfied; he will not complain about any suffering: "Why do I have to face this?" – He will gladly bear also in this visible life what is his due. – After death he is imprisoned by his self; he sees no way out while suffering great agonies. He cannot think anything else than that he must suffer: "I have earned this; I suffer gladly." When he then remembers to tell himself: "I thank you, Father, for letting me atone for my sins like this" – he can then lift his gaze upwards, and light comes for him. He is amazed; it feels all too good; and when he looks he sees Jesus. Jesus stands there infinitely good and smiling, forgiving. And the soul feels within, not that Jesus would accept his sins, but he feels limitless joy for the fact that he can overcome his sins. And he storms out of his prison along the path of light to the master.

This is miraculous; and of course it happens to quite many, but still only to those who really follow Jesus Christ and have understood his teachings here on Earth. – Many, many Christians sit in their prisons and when they are explained, they cannot listen; they just agonize until they are shouted to again and again: "Wake up and see how things are!" Only then they will gradually calm down and be liberated. – Usually those who follow Jesus do not end up in such condition. They suffer so much internally here on Earth that they do not have that any more after death – but occasionally it could be so too. A person does not always know himself; there might be something in him of which he is not fully aware of, and that he must deal with after death for there can be no evil in heaven.

Then, when a person in heaven receives an inner knowledge that: "Now I must go back on Earth" – he will be lead into a great light. It is like entering a marvellous hall. He forgets everything and feels as if he were an atom in the universe. He comes as if into a diamond hall; a wondrous book is read to him which contains his incarnations. And then there opens up before him the life in which he must go to. And he is filled with great joy that he can attend the school of God, can advance, and be a part of it all. With joy he promises God: "I want to aspire with all my power, I give all my life!" – He will then forget all this on Earth but in his soul will resound a voice: "You must do this; you must give up that." For in this very personality resounds the voice of man's own exalted spiritual self and knowledge.